Critical Acclaim for *PC Learning Labs Teaches WordPerfect 5.1*

"...a tightly focused book that doesn't stray from its purpose...it concentrates on the beginner, and it stays with the beginner."

—William J. Lynott, *Online Today*

PC Learning Labs

TEACHES
WORDPERFECT
5.1

Ziff-Davis Press

Emeryville, California

PC Learning Labs

TEACHES
WORDPERFECT
5.1

Logical Operations

Writer	Robert Nichols Kulik
Series Editor	Eric Stone
Copy Editor	David Peal
Technical Reviewers	Mark D. Hall and Dick Hol
Project Coordinator	Ami Knox
Proofreader	Sylvia Townsend
Cover Design	Ken Roberts
Series Design Concept	Collins Flannery
Book Design	Laura Lamar/MAX, San Francisco
Series Illustration	Peter Tucker and Tony Jonick
Technical Illustration	Cherie Plumlee and Stephen Bradshaw
Word Processing	Howard Blechman and Kim Haglund
Page Layout	Tony Jonick, Anna L. Marks, and Bruce Lundquist
Indexer	Elinor Lindheimer

This book was produced on a Macintosh IIfx, with the following applications: FrameMaker®, Microsoft® Word, MacLink® *Plus*, Aldus® FreeHand™, and Collage Plus™.

Ziff-Davis Press
5903 Christie Avenue
Emeryville, CA 94608

ISBN 1-56276-032-7
10 9 8 7 6

CONTENTS AT A GLANCE

TABLE OF CONTENTS

INTRODUCTION

Welcome to *PC Learning Labs Teaches WordPerfect 5.1*. You are about to embark on a unique journey. When you come to the end of this journey, you will have learned all the basic skills necessary to use WordPerfect 5.1, one of the most popular and most sophisticated word-processing programs available today. You will then be able to take this knowledge and apply it directly to your own work— wherever you work and whatever you do.

This book is unique in that it incorporates what we at PC Learning Labs have learned from years of teaching WordPerfect in a classroom setting. We've used our experience in the classroom to create documents that will enable you to learn WordPerfect on a computer at your home or office. Unlike a class, this book encourages you to proceed at your own pace. Furthermore, we've carefully chosen the order of the topics to make sure you are always applying and reinforcing what you learned in earlier, more basic topics.

On this journey, you will be guided every step of the way, and you'll be shown landmarks so that you can chart your own progress and be confident in knowing that you're on a steady course. We hope that you find all the material in this book useful, informative, and fun.

WHO THIS BOOK IS FOR

This book starts you off with basic word-processing skills. For this reason, we assume that you have little or no experience with Word-Perfect or even with computers. Even if you have been using Word-Perfect or another word processor for some time, we trust that our systematic approach will provide you with a detailed, thorough, and practical knowledge of the program.

WHAT YOU NEED

This book assumes that your computer has a hard disk and that you have installed WordPerfect 5.1 on it. If you have not yet installed WordPerfect, see Appendix A for guidance. We will not assume that you have a printer, though readers who do have a printer will learn how to put it to work. We also will not assume that you have a mouse; everything you need to accomplish in WordPerfect 5.1 can be done easily through the keyboard.

WHAT THIS BOOK CONTAINS

Only the application, continued practice, and exploration of the material in this book will result in your eventual mastery of Word-Perfect 5.1. This book facilitates and supports your initial and continued learning by including the following components:

- Carefully sequenced topics, designed to build on the knowledge you've gained from previous topics.

- Hands-on activities, through which you are guided step by step. In these activities, each step and keystroke is clearly given, and the results of performing that step are clearly explained.

- Illustrations that show how your screen should look at key points along the way.

- "Practice Your Skills" sections, which are challenging activities that apply the skills taught in one or more chapters. These activities, placed at strategically located points, help you to incorporate and apply many of your new skills in a broader context.

- Chapter summaries, which recap the major techniques covered in each chapter in a two-column format that's ideal for quick reference.

- A *Data Disk*, which contains all the files you will need to work through this course at a computer.

HOW TO USE THIS BOOK AS A LEARNING TOOL

Each chapter in this book is complete; it covers one broad skill or a set of closely related skills. Chapters are arranged by skill level, meaning that techniques learned in earlier chapters are used later on when more complex topics are covered. For this reason, you should go through chapters in the order they are presented. If a chapter covers material with which you are already familiar, you might want to work through it to reinforce a skill that you already possess.

You get to try out each new technique on a document that's already been prepared for you. This saves you typing time and allows you to concentrate on the technique at hand. Through the use of these documents, the hands-on activities, the illustrations that give you feedback at each crucial step of the way, and the supporting background information, this book provides you with the foundation and structure to learn WordPerfect.

The amount of material you cover in any given session is strictly up to you. After all, you've chosen the self-study approach, and you should be the best judge of what you need. In general it helps not to try to absorb too much information at one time. In fact, studies have shown that most people assimilate and retain information when it is presented in digestible chunks and is followed by a liberal amount of practice.

HOW TO USE THIS BOOK AS A TOOL FOR REVIEW

A method of instruction can only be as effective as the continued practice you are willing to invest in it. For this reason, we strongly recommend that you review and work through any of the topics and activities presented in this book. How much material you cover before reviewing is up to you. You might review a series of steps within an activity, a complete activity, an entire topic, a series of topics, or one or more chapters. Whichever method you choose, this book has been designed so that you can go back over any of the material any number of times.

Most topics open with a bulleted list presenting the salient points or actions, and serving as a handy future reference. In your own work at home or at the office, you might from time to time forget the order of steps in a procedure and need to be reminded of the correct basic sequence. In this case, rather than go back over a detailed activity, you might want to review the points summarized in the bulleted list *before* the activity.

HOW TO USE THIS BOOK AS A QUICK REFERENCE

The same features that make this book handy as a tool for review also make it invaluable as a quick reference. Topics are presented clearly and concisely, so there is no extraneous information. You will always know where discussion of a topic begins and ends. Whenever possible, cross-references are given to other topics and chapters so that you can quickly look up any related skills or techniques. Also, every chapter ends with a two-column quick reference that lists the techniques presented in that chapter and the keys you need to press to apply them.

USING THE DATA DISK

One of the most important features of this book is the Data Disk. This disk contains the sample files you'll retrieve and work on throughout this book. These are specially created documents, designed to give you a foundation that you will build upon as you acquire new skills. To perform most of the activities in this book, you will retrieve the original sample document file from this disk and make changes to it. When you save the file, you will rename it and save it to your C:\WP51 directory (the directory that also contains the WordPerfect 5.1 program). The original document will remain intact on the Data Disk for future use.

Before you begin, you should make a copy of your Data Disk, so that you'll have a backup in case something happens to the original disk. To do this:

1. Turn on your computer. (Follow the instructions in your computer manual.)

2. After you see the screen prompt C>, C:>, C:\>, or something similar, type **diskcopy a: a:** and press **Enter**. You will see the prompt

```
Insert SOURCE diskette in drive A:
Press any key when ready . . .
```

3. Insert your Data Disk in drive A of your computer, close the drive door (if necessary), and press any key. After a short time, you will see the prompt

```
Insert TARGET diskette in drive A:
Press any key when ready . . .
```

4. Remove the Data Disk from drive A, and replace it with a formatted blank disk. Close the drive door (if necessary).

5. Press any key. The contents of the Data Disk are now being copied to the blank disk. After the copying is completed, you see the prompt

```
Copy another diskette? Y/N
```

6. Press **N** (No).

7. Remove the disk and remember to label it and cover the write-protect notch. Use your copy to key through this book, and store the original Data Disk in a safe place, preferably one that is cool and dry.

A QUICK GUIDE TO THE KEYBOARD

Computers come with various different styles of keyboards. These keyboards work in the same way, but the layout of the keys varies somewhat from keyboard to keyboard. Figures I.1, I.2, and I.3 show the three main styles of keyboard and how their keys are arranged.

WordPerfect 5.1 uses three main areas of the keyboard, as shown in Figures I.1 through I.3:

- The *function keys*, F1 through F10 or F12, enable you to use many of WordPerfect's features. On the PC- and XT/AT-style keyboards there are 10 such keys located at the left end of the keyboard; on the PS/2-style Enhanced Keyboard there are 12, located across the top of the keyboard. (Note: The function keys F11 and F12 are not necessary in order to use WordPerfect.)

- The *typing keys*, or *alphanumeric* keys, are located in the center of all keyboards. These are the letter, number, and punctuation keys, like those found on a common typewriter.

- The *numeric keypad* conveniently groups the numbers 0 through 9, which are also found across the top row of the typing keys, in one compact area for easier entry. The numeric keypad also contains the cursor-movement keys. Press the Num Lock key to switch between numeric entry and cursor movement. (For the use of the cursor-movement keys, see Chapter 1.) On the Enhanced Keyboard, there is a separate, additional cursor-movement keypad.

Figure I.1   The IBM PC–style keyboard

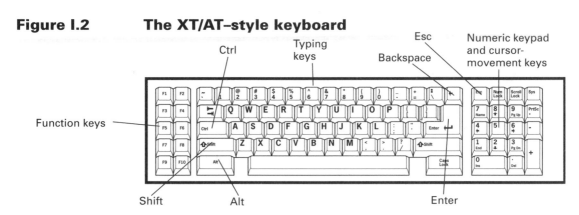

Figure I.2   The XT/AT–style keyboard

Figure I.3   The PS/2–style Enhanced Keyboard

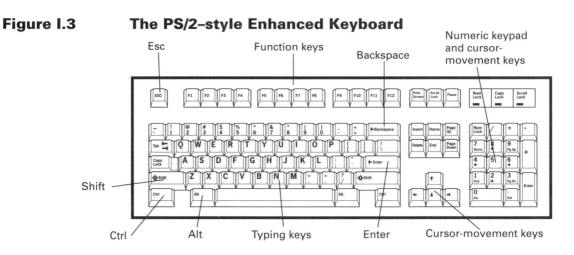

The typing keyboard includes the Ctrl, Shift, and Alt keys. To access WordPerfect's many features, you will use these keys alone or in combination with one of these three keys. The Ctrl, Shift, and Alt keys don't do anything if you press them without pressing another key. If you are familiar with the use of a typewriter, then you'll already be familiar with the Shift key's most common use—creating uppercase letters and other special characters. You will become familiar with the uses of most of the individual keys as you progress through this book.

CONVENTIONS USED IN THIS BOOK

In activities that you are to perform at a computer, keystrokes, menu choices, and any characters you are to type are presented in boldface. Here's an example:

1. Press **F8** (Underline).

2. Type **Introduction**. The text is underlined.

3. Press **Ctrl-F8** (Font) to display the Font menu. Choose **2 A**ppearance; then choose **2 U**ndln to turn underlining off.

4. Press **Enter** to end the line.

To help you distinguish between steps presented for your general knowledge and steps you should carry out at your computer as you read, we have adopted the following system:

- A bulleted step, like this, is provided for your information and reference only.

1. A numbered step, like this, indicates one of a series of steps that you should carry out in sequence at your computer.

Another convention in this book is the use of a hyphen (-) to show that you should press more than one key. For example, *Ctrl-F3* means that you *press and hold* the Ctrl key, then press F3, then release them both. The hyphen is used in this way with the Ctrl, Shift, and Alt keys. In contrast, strings of keys that are pressed and released *before* the next key is pressed are separated by commas. For example *Home, Home, Home,* ↑ means to press and release Home three times, then press the Up Arrow key.

WordPerfect offers you an abundance of features to help you create, enhance, and edit text. This book shows you how to use these features to improve the content of your documents and the way they look. Welcome to WordPerfect, welcome to this book, and have fun!

CHAPTER ONE: WORDPERFECT BASICS

Starting
WordPerfect

The Basics of
Entering Text

Editing a
Document

Saving, Naming,
and Printing a
Document

Clearing the Typing
Area

If you've ever used a typewriter to create a document, you know that it's easy to make mistakes. Because letters are committed to paper as you compose the text, even simple typing changes like erasing a letter can become difficult. More extensive corrections generally require that you retype the entire document.

A *word processor* like WordPerfect provides you with a much more efficient way of creating, revising, and saving a document, because you can edit it and even make major adjustments, such as changing the margins or page breaks, in a single step or series of steps. Then, once you're satisfied with the appearance and content of your document, you can print it.

This chapter covers procedures that are essential to effective word processing. You will encounter most of them each time you use WordPerfect. When you have finished this chapter, you will be able to:

- Enter text
- Use the Tab and Enter keys
- Edit a document by inserting, deleting, and replacing text
- Save, name, and print a document
- Clear the typing area
- Exit a document
- Open and close menus

STARTING WORDPERFECT

Before you start WordPerfect, the program should be installed on your hard disk. See Appendix A if you need help installing the program. Also, you will be using the Data Disk, the disk provided with this book. The Data Disk contains the prepared document files used throughout this book.

Follow these steps:

1. Turn on your computer.

2. If prompted for the date, type today's date. (Skip to Step 4 if you are not prompted for the date.) Use the month-day-year format with dashes or slashes: *mm-dd-yy* or *mm/dd/yy*.

3. Press **Enter**. After typing a command, you must press Enter. Only then is the command actually carried out.

4. If prompted for the time, type the current time. (Skip to Step 6 if you are not prompted for the time.) Use the hour-minute format with a colon as separator, *hh:mm*.

5. Press **Enter**.

6. Insert the Data Disk in drive A of your computer.

7. Type **c:\wp51\wp**. This command tells DOS where to find Word-Perfect (the C:\WP51 directory) and issues the command to start the program (WP). If you installed WordPerfect in a directory other than WP51, use that directory name instead of WP51 in this step.

8. Press **Enter**.

After WordPerfect has loaded into the computer's memory, your screen should resemble the one shown in Figure 1.1.

Figure 1.1   **The WordPerfect typing area**

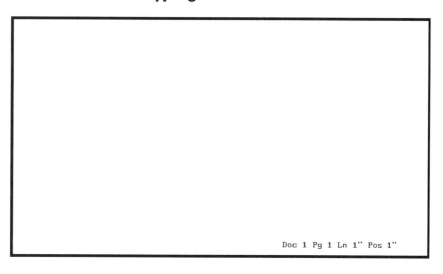

Doc 1 Pg 1 Ln 1" Pos 1"

THE BASICS OF ENTERING TEXT

When you start WordPerfect, it displays a blank screen called the *typing area*, where the text you type appears. Formatting codes (which control text effects such as bold, underline, center, indent, and tab) are hidden from view unless you want to see them. Chapter 4 tells you more about codes.

THE STATUS LINE

The *status line* appears at the bottom of the WordPerfect typing area: It is an information center that is always present while you are working in a document. The right-hand side of the status line identifies the location of the *cursor*, the movable flashing line or rectangle that shows where the next character you type will appear on your screen. The status line summarizes your cursor's location, as shown in Table 1.1.

Table 1.1   **Status Line Indicators**

Status Line Indicator	Purpose
DOC	Identifies the document you are working in. In WordPerfect you can edit two documents at the same time. *DOC* will read either *1* or *2*.
PAGE	Indicates the page number within the active document.
LN	Indicates the line your cursor is on, measured in inches from the top of the page.
POS	Indicates the cursor's location on a line, measured in inches from the left-hand side of the page.

Follow these steps at your computer:

1. Notice that the position indicator, Pos, appears as a combination of uppercase and lowercase letters. The current cursor position should be *1*", meaning that the cursor is located one inch from the left edge of the page.

2. Type your first name. Notice that all letters are lowercase.

3. Take another look at the Pos indicator. It indicates that your cursor has changed position.

4. Press **Caps Lock**. Now look at the position indicator. It should read *POS*—all uppercase letters—because you pressed Caps Lock.

5. With Caps Lock still turned on, type your first name. The position indicator should still read *POS*. The letters of your name now appear in uppercase. Note that pressing and holding the Shift key as you type produces *lowercase* letters, despite the fact that Caps Lock is turned on. Also note that the number—and therefore the cursor position—has changed again.

6. If the POS indicator is flashing, press **Num Lock**.

7. Press ← on the *numeric keypad*, the group of keys on the right-hand side of most keyboards. The cursor moved one character to the left. Note that the position indicator reflects the cursor's new position.

8. Press → on the numeric keypad. The cursor moved one character to the right.

9. Press **Num Lock**. Notice that the POS indicator is now flashing. This is WordPerfect's way of telling you that Num Lock is turned on.

10. With Num Lock still turned on, press ← on the numeric keypad. Then, press →. Instead of changing your cursor position, you typed the digits **46**. This happened because Num Lock activates the numeric keypad: Pressing those keys will display numbers on the screen instead of moving the cursor.

11. Press **Backspace**. Notice that doing so deletes the character to the *left* of the cursor. Continue pressing the **Backspace** key until you have deleted all the text you have just typed. (Note that the Delete or Del key erases characters in the other direction, from left to right.)

12. Press **Caps Lock** *and* **Num Lock**. Caps Lock and Num Lock are *toggles*—they turn the respective features on and off. Press either key once to turn on the feature, and press again to turn it off. Also note that Pos (with a capital *P* and small *os*) is now displayed, and it no longer flashes. This tells you that both Caps Lock and Num Lock are turned off.

Here's a helpful hint: If your keyboard has a separate arrow keypad (often placed between the main key section and the numeric keypad), it's best to use that keyboard to move the cursor. That way, you won't accidentally type numbers with the numeric keypad.

 USING THE ENTER KEY

In word processing, the Enter key is sometimes called the Return key, a term based on the similarity of the Enter key to the carriage *return* on a typewriter. In word processing, unlike typing, you do not press Enter at the end of each line. When text does not fit on a line, WordPerfect "wraps" words to the beginning of the next line. This feature is called *word-wrap*. Chapter 7 will show you how to control word-wrap by setting margins, and Chapter 8 will show you how to use WordPerfect's Hyphenation feature to fine-tune your control over where a line ends.

The only times you'll need to press Enter are

- To end a short line—a line that ends before the right margin is reached

- To end a paragraph

- To insert a blank line

On a clear WordPerfect screen, follow these steps:

1. Type **John Martinson**.

2. Press **Enter** to end the line and move the cursor to the beginning of the next line.

3. Type **2345 Industrial Circle** and press **Enter**.

4. Type **Nashua, NH 03060** and press **Enter**.

5. Press **Enter** to add another blank line.

6. Type **Dear Ted:** and press **Enter** *twice*, once to end the line and once more to skip a blank line.

Remember: If you make any minor errors while typing, you can always press Backspace to correct them.

 USING THE TAB KEY

Tabs, or tab stops, are positions that you can set on a line. Tabs make it easier to indent a line or whole paragraph, to create tables, and to position the cursor on a line. Pressing Tab moves the cursor to the next tab stop. In WordPerfect, tab stops are normally set at every half inch. (Chapter 6 will tell you how to adjust tab stops.)

Follow these steps at your computer:

1. Press **Tab** to position the cursor at the first tab stop.

2. Press **Tab** twice to move the cursor two more tab stops to the right.

3. Press **Backspace** twice to move the cursor to the left, erasing the two new inserted tabs.

4. Type the first sentence as shown in Figure 1.2 and press **Spacebar** twice.

5. Type **Orders are picking up in every region**. You will notice that WordPerfect breaks to the next line automatically as you type, as a result of word-wrap.

Figure 1.2   **A sample WordPerfect document**

```
John Martinson
2345 Industrial Circle
Nashua, NH 03060

Dear Ted:

     Please find our first quarter sales report enclosed.  Orders are picking
up in every region.  Your region posted a terrific gain of twelve percent.

     I have enclosed the agenda for the quarterly meeting.  I look ahead to
seeing all of you again at that time.  Keep up the good work!

Yours truly,


(Your name)




                                                Doc 1 Pg 1 Ln 3.67" Pos 1"
```

6. Complete the letter as shown in Figure 1.2. When you come to the end of a paragraph, press **Enter** twice.

EDITING A DOCUMENT

You've already seen that word processing can make it easier to create and navigate your way through documents. Word processing is especially useful as an aid in editing documents. For example, on a typewriter, if you realize that you've omitted a word after typing a line of text, you can't go back and insert it—at least not without smearing White-Out on the page. It's also difficult to delete or replace text. With a word processor, you can easily insert, delete, move, and copy text. All text after your changes automatically adjusts to them.

Before you do any editing, let's get more experience using arrow keys to move around in a document. Using the same letter you were working on in the previous section, follow the next steps at your computer.

1. Press ↑ several times. Each time you press the key, the cursor moves up one line.

2. Press ↓ several times to move the cursor down one line at a time. Position the cursor on a line containing text.

3. Press → several times to move the cursor to the right one character at a time.

4. Press ← several times to move the cursor to the left one character at a time.

 INSERTING TEXT

WordPerfect is normally in the *Insert* mode. As you type, text to the right of the cursor is pushed farther right, rather than overwritten (replaced). To insert text, use the arrow keys to position the cursor where you would like to begin inserting text in the document, and type.

Follow these steps at your computer:

1. Use the arrow keys to move the cursor under the *K* in *Keep*, in the last sentence of the second paragraph. This is where you will insert the new text.

2. Type

   In the meantime,

   and press the Spacebar to leave a space after the new phrase. The existing text was pushed to the right of the text being typed. While in the Insert mode, you don't have to press any special keys to insert text in the document. Compare your screen to Figure 1.3.

 DELETING TEXT

The Backspace key deletes the single character or code (such as a tab stop) immediately to the *left* of the cursor. The Del key deletes the character directly *above* the cursor (that is, the character *on* which the cursor is blinking). You can use either of these keys to delete text one character at a time. Try not to get in the habit of holding down the Backspace key; otherwise you may delete too much text inadvertently.

Follow these steps at your computer:

1. Use the arrow keys to move the cursor under the *K* in *Keep*.

2. Press **Del** to delete the text at the cursor. Notice that the capital *K* in *Keep* is deleted.

Figure 1.3   **Letter with inserted text**

```
John Martinson
2345 Industrial Circle
Nashua, NH 03060

Dear Ted:

     Please find our first quarter sales report enclosed.  Orders
are picking up in every region.  Your region posted a terrific gain
of twelve percent.

     I have enclosed the agenda for the quarterly meeting.  I look
ahead to seeing all of you again at that time.  In the meantime, Keep up the goo
work!

Yours truly,

(Your name)




                                      Doc 1 Pg 1 Ln 2.83" Pos 7.5"
```

3. Type **k** to change the word to *keep*.

4. Move the cursor so that it is under the space after the word *Circle*, in the second line of the address.

5. Press **Backspace** six times to delete the six letters of the word *Circle*. Backspace deletes the character to the left of the cursor.

6. Type **Parkway**. The inside address should now read *2345 Industrial Parkway*, as seen in Figure 1.4.

TYPEOVER MODE

The alternative to using Insert mode, described in the previous section, is *Typeover* mode, in which new text overwrites, or types over, old text directly in its path. To activate Typeover mode, press the Ins key.

```
Typeover
```

appears on the left-hand side of the status line, and Typeover mode remains in effect until you press Ins again to return to Insert mode.

A word of caution: Despite its apparent convenience, Typeover mode should be used as little as possible, if at all. Because it's easy to forget that you've turned on Typeover mode, you might think that you're inserting text when you are actually overwriting text that you wanted to keep.

Figure 1.4   **Letter after deleting and inserting text**

```
John Martinson
2345 Industrial Parkway
Nashua, NH 03060

Dear Ted:

     Please find our first quarter sales report enclosed.   Orders
are picking up in every region.   Your region posted a terrific gain
of twelve percent.

     I have enclosed the agenda for the quarterly meeting.   I look
ahead to seeing all of you again at that time.   In the meantime,
keep up the good work!

Yours truly,

(Your name)




                                          Doc 1 Pg 1 Ln 1.17" Pos 3.3"
```

Follow these steps at your computer:

1. Move the cursor so that it is under the *p* in *picking up,* in the second sentence of the first paragraph.

2. Press **Ins**. The status line reads *Typeover.* You are now in Type-over mode.

3. Type the word **increasing**. Notice that *picking up* is replaced by *increasing.*

4. Press **Ins**. You are now back in Insert mode.

PRACTICE YOUR SKILLS

Use the skills you've just learned to complete the corrections listed below and shown in Figure 1.5.

1. Delete *Ted* and type **John**.

2. Delete the word *our* in the first sentence of the first paragraph and type **the**.

3. Delete *ahead* in the second sentence of the second paragraph and type **forward**.

4. Delete *Yours truly* and type **Sincerely**.

Figure 1.5 **Delete struck-out text and insert bold text**

```
John Martinson
2345 Industrial Circle Parkway
Nashua, NH 03060

Dear Ted John:

     Please find our the first quarter sales report enclosed.
Orders are picking-up increasing in every region.  Your region
posted a terrific gain of twelve percent.

     I have enclosed the agenda for the quarterly meeting.  I
look ahead forward to seeing all of you again at that time.  In
the meantime, Keep keep up the good work!

Yours truly Sincerely,


(Your name)
```

5. Delete *terrific* in the third sentence of the first paragraph. Also delete the trailing blank space after *terrific*.

Check your work against the letter shown in Figure 1.6.

Figure 1.6 **The corrected letter**

```
John Martinson
2345 Industrial Parkway
Nashua NH  03060

Dear John:

     Please find the first quarter sales report enclosed.  Orders
are increasing in every region.  Your region posted a gain of
twelve percent.

     I have enclosed the agenda for the quarterly meeting.  I look
forward to seeing all of you again at that time.  In the meantime,
keep up the good work!

Sincerely,


(Your name)
```

SAVING, NAMING, AND PRINTING A DOCUMENT

Until you save a document, it exists only in computer *memory*, a temporary storage place that is available only as long as the power is on. When the power is turned off, your computer's memory empties; all your active files are erased. By copying all your files onto a disk (your computer's hard disk or a removable 3½- or 5¼-inch disk), you can later retrieve and alter them. You can think of a disk as a storage area more permanent than your computer's memory.

Get in the habit of saving your work frequently. That way, if something happens to the document in memory, you will have a recent copy of the document on disk, so that retyping will be kept to a minimum. Remember, if you make changes to a recently saved document, your changes will not be stored until you save the file with those changes.

Here are some helpful suggestions for saving your work:

- Save every 15 minutes.

- Save before printing. Otherwise, only the most recently saved copy will print.

- Save before spell-checking. Chapter 8 tells you how to use WordPerfect's spell-checker.

- Save from your hard disk to a removable disk at the end of a WordPerfect session.

NAMING A DOCUMENT: SOME CONVENTIONS

If you are saving a document for the first time, you must name it. Later, you use this name to retrieve the document. To name a document, it is a good idea to follow these conventions:

- File names may contain up to eight characters.

- File names may include all letters or numbers, or a combination of both. Case is not significant.

- File names may not contain spaces or punctuation marks (except - , _ , and .).

- File names should be descriptive, so that a name reflects a file's contents.

- No two file names may be the same.

- An *extension* of one to three characters can be added to the file name, if you wish. Giving different files the same extension can help you keep track of your documents. If you add an extension, you must separate it from the file name with a period (for exam-ple, LETTER.LRN).

SAVE AND EXIT

There are two ways to save a document: Save and Exit.

- The Save key, F10, transfers a copy of the document from com-puter memory to disk, while allowing you to remain in the doc-ument and work on it.

- The Exit key, F7, copies the file to the disk and removes the doc-ument from the typing area. F7 also gives you the choice of ed-iting another document or exiting WordPerfect.

When the document in the typing area has been saved, the file name and location (*path*) are displayed on the left-hand side of the status line.

Follow these steps at your computer:

1. Press **F10** to save the letter you have been working on. The prompt line reads

```
Document to be saved:
```

It is asking you to name the document.

2. Type

```
myletter.lrn
```

The file name is MYLETTER (eight characters), and the exten-sion is LRN (three characters). Press **Enter**. (The file is not saved until you press Enter.) The following message appears

```
Saving C:\WP51\MYLETTER.LRN
```

A copy of the file is written to the disk, yet the document re-mains in the typing area for you to work on.

3. Observe the file name and path display

```
C:\WP51\MYLETTER.LRN
```

on the far-left of the status line. Notice that even though you typed the file name in lowercase letters, the name is automati-cally saved in uppercase.

WORKING WITH MENUS AND OPTIONS

A menu is a list of choices, or options, related to a function. Menus give you choices for doing such things as formatting a page or printing a document. Figure 1.7 shows all the choices available on the Print menu. In WordPerfect, there are two ways to choose menu options:

- Type the corresponding number of the menu choice.

- Type the underscored or highlighted letter (often the first letter of the feature).

Figure 1.7 **The WordPerfect Print and Options menu**

```
Print

      1 - Full Document
      2 - Page
      3 - Document on Disk
      4 - Control Printer
      5 - Multiple Pages
      6 - View Document
      7 - Initialize Printer


Options

      S - Select Printer                  Epson FX-80/100
      B - Binding Offset                  0"
      N - Number of Copies                1
      U - Multiple Copies Generated by    WordPerfect
      G - Graphics Quality                Medium
      T - Text Quality                    High



Selection: 0
```

To get out of any menu that you no longer want to use, press the Cancel key, F1. You will be returned to your last position—either the typing area or the previous menu.

The Exit key, F7, also lets you leave a menu. Unlike F1, F7 always returns you directly to the typing area. Also, while F1 cancels any menu selections you've made, F7 puts them into effect.

Follow these steps at your computer:

1. Press **Shift-F7** to display the **Print** menu (Figure 1.7). The printer name in the right-hand column of the Print menu will probably differ from the one shown in the figure. Also, you may see additional options if you are running WordPerfect on a network.

2. Examine the menu choices. Remember that you can select a menu option by pressing either its number or the bold letter in its name.

3. Press **F1** to leave the menu and return to the typing area.

Note: Whenever you are using a two-key combination, it is important to *hold down* the first key (Shift, Ctrl, or Alt) while pressing the second key. Then release both keys. If you accidentally release the first key before pressing the second one, you will bring up the wrong menu or issue the wrong command. If this happens, press F1 to cancel the command, and start again.

PRINTING A DOCUMENT

WordPerfect allows you to print in the *background:* You can continue editing documents while printing. You can even edit the same document that is printing, but the changes will not be reflected in that printout. However, when you edit or create while printing, the program responds more slowly.

To print a document, follow these general steps:

- Save the document.

- Press Shift-F7.

- Choose 1 - Full Document from the menu. This will print the entire document.

WordPerfect normally prints documents with full justification. (*Justified* text has an even right margin, rather than a ragged one.) WordPerfect is also set up to print with right, left, top, and bottom margins of 1 inch. Procedures for changing these settings are given in Chapters 3, 6, and 7.

Follow these steps at your computer:

1. Press **Shift-F7** to display the **Print** and **Options** menu (Figure 1.7).

2. Choose **1 - F**ull Document from the Print menu. Remember that you can continue working without waiting for the document to print.

CLEARING THE TYPING AREA

Once you've finished working in a document, and before you start working in a different one, you should clear the typing area. Otherwise, WordPerfect will insert the new document into the current one (the one that has not been cleared), combining the two files in the typing area. (On occasion, you may want to combine short documents into a large one using this technique.)

As you've already seen, F7 can be used to save a copy of the file in memory and clear the typing area. You can then begin typing a new document or retrieve an existing file to work on (as explained in Chapter 2).

To use Exit to clear the typing area:

- Press F7. WordPerfect prompts

  `Save document?`

- Type Y.

- Type the name of the document, or press Enter to accept the displayed name (if you have already saved this document).

- If WordPerfect prompts

  `Replace <filename>?`

  type Y to update the file.

- When WordPerfect prompts

  `Exit WP?`

  type N to clear the typing area. If you type Y here, you will exit WordPerfect.

  When WordPerfect prompts

  `Exit WP?`

  press F1 to return to the document, *if* you want to do more work.

Follow these steps at your computer to save the document now on your screen:

1. Press **F7** to exit. WordPerfect prompts

   `Save document? Yes (No)`

2. Type **Y** for *Yes.* (If you were to type **N** here, the file would not be saved.) WordPerfect prompts

   ```
   Document to be saved: C:\WP51\MYLETTER.LRN
   ```

3. Press **Enter** to save the document MYLETTER.LRN. WordPerfect prompts

   ```
   Replace C:\WP51\MYLETTER.LRN?  No (Yes)
   ```

4. Type **Y** to update the file MYLETTER.LRN on disk with the copy of the file in memory. Notice the message that is displayed

   ```
   Saving C:\WP51\MYLETTER.LRN
   ```

   followed by the prompt

   ```
   Exit WP? No (Yes)
   ```

5. Type **N** for *No* if you want to remain in WordPerfect or **Y** to return to the DOS prompt.

Pressing Enter or any key other than Y keeps you in the program and clears the typing area. Typing Y brings you back to the DOS prompt, ending the work session.

CHAPTER SUMMARY

Congratulations! In this first chapter, you've learned the essential procedures that you'll be using in the following chapters of this book and in your day-to-day experience with WordPerfect. You've learned the basics of entering text, reading and interpreting the status line, and using the Enter and Tab keys. You've also learned some important editing techniques: inserting, deleting, and replacing text; saving, naming, and printing your work; and clearing the typing area.

Here's a quick technique reference for Chapter 1:

Feature or Action	How to Do It
Start WordPerfect	At the DOS prompt, type **c:\wp51\wp**, then press **Enter**
Type in uppercase letters	**Caps Lock**
Move the cursor left, one character at a time	←

Feature or Action	How to Do It
Move one character to the right	$\rightarrow$
Create a blank line	**Enter**
Move to the first (or next) tab stop	**Tab**
Move up one line at a time	$\uparrow$
Move down one line at a time	$\downarrow$
Erase the character above (at) the cursor	**Del**
Erase the character (or tab) to the left of the cursor	**Backspace**
Replace (overwrite) text	**Ins** (Typeover mode)
Save and name a file without exiting the document	**F10**
Save and exit a document	**F7**
Display the **Print** menu	**Shift-F7**
Print the entire document (from the Print menu)	**1-**Full Document
Cancel a command	**F1**

In the next chapter, you will learn the following skills: retrieving a document from a list of files; moving around in a document; deleting large portions of text; searching for text; and using WordPerfect's Search and Replace features.

CHAPTER TWO: WORKING IN LARGE DOCUMENTS

The basic skills you learned in Chapter 1 allow you to move around in a small document and do some minor editing. But on a larger document, you will need faster, more efficient ways to do your work. For example, suppose that you are working on a 23-page report and need to move quickly to page 22 and delete a large block of text. You could, of course, use the skills you have already learned and move a line at a time. However, with the shortcuts in this chapter, you'll be able to do your work in much less time.

By the time you are finished with this chapter, you will know how to:

- Retrieve a document

- Move around in a large document

- Delete large portions of text

- Undelete (restore) something you have just deleted

- Search for specific information in a document

- Search for specific information and replace it with new information

- Save a document under a new name

RETRIEVING A DOCUMENT

There are times when you want to retrieve a document from a disk but can't remember the file name. To solve this problem, WordPerfect provides a very useful feature, List Files.

The List Files key, F5, enables you to retrieve a file from a disk and place the text in the typing area. It also lets you perform a variety of tasks by highlighting a file name and selecting an option. You'll be learning about these tasks in this and later chapters.

To view a list of files, press F5. A directory name appears in the lower-left corner of the typing area (for example, C:\WP51*.*). This name tells you the drive and directory whose contents will be viewed in the List Files area. In WordPerfect, the default, or normal, setting is C:\WP51*.*. To accept the highlighted directory, press Enter. To select a different directory, type the drive and directory over the default (for example, A:\documents), and then press Enter.

Place the Data Disk in drive A and follow these steps at your computer:

1. With the typing area cleared, examine your screen. The typing area should always be empty before you retrieve a file.

2. Press **F5**, the List Files key. The prompt probably displays

   `Dir C:\WP51\*.* (Type = to change default Dir)`

3. Type **A:** to change to drive A.

4. Press **Enter** to accept the displayed directory name (path). A screen like the one shown in Figure 2.1 appears.

Figure 2.1 **The List Files screen**

Date and time display

Directory reference

Free disk space

Used disk space

Number of files in directory

Size of the document in memory

File information

Options

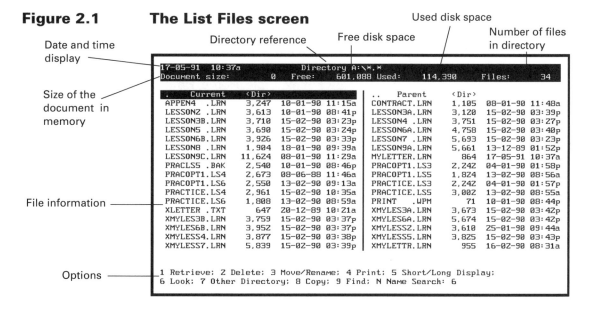

```
17-05-91  10:37a            Directory A:\*.*
Document size:      0   Free:    601,088 Used:    114,390    Files:    34

.    Current   <Dir>                  ..    Parent    <Dir>
APPEN4  .LRN    3,247  10-01-90 11:15a  CONTRACT.LRN    1,105  08-01-90 11:48a
LESSON2 .LRN    3,613  10-01-90 08:41p  LESSON3A.LRN    3,120  15-02-90 03:39p
LESSON3B.LRN    3,710  15-02-90 03:23p  LESSON4 .LRN    3,751  15-02-90 03:27p
LESSON5 .LRN    3,690  15-02-90 03:24p  LESSON6A.LRN    4,758  15-02-90 03:40p
LESSON6B.LRN    3,926  15-02-90 03:33p  LESSON7 .LRN    5,693  15-02-90 03:23p
LESSON8 .LRN    1,904  18-01-90 09:39a  LESSON9A.LRN    5,661  13-12-89 01:52p
LESSON9C.LRN   11,624  08-01-90 11:29a  MYLETTER.LRN      864  17-05-91 10:37a
PRACLS5 .BAK    2,540  10-01-90 08:46p  PRACOPT1.LS3    2,242  04-01-90 01:58p
PRACOPT1.LS4    2,673  08-06-88 11:46a  PRACOPT1.LS5    1,824  13-02-90 08:56a
PRACOPT1.LS6    2,550  13-02-90 09:13a  PRACTICE.LS3    2,242  04-01-90 01:57p
PRACTICE.LS4    2,961  15-02-90 10:35a  PRACTICE.LS5    3,002  13-02-90 08:55a
PRACTICE.LS6    1,808  13-02-90 08:59a  PRINT   .WPM       71  10-01-90 08:44p
XLETTER .TXT      647  20-12-89 10:21a  XMYLES3A.LRN    3,673  15-02-90 03:42p
XMYLES3B.LRN    3,759  15-02-90 03:37p  XMYLES6A.LRN    5,674  15-02-90 03:42p
XMYLES6B.LRN    3,952  15-02-90 03:37p  XMYLESS2.LRN    3,610  25-01-90 09:44a
XMYLESS4.LRN    3,877  15-02-90 03:38p  XMYLESS5.LRN    3,825  15-02-90 03:43p
XMYLESS7.LRN    5,839  15-02-90 03:39p  XMYLETTR.LRN      955  16-02-90 08:31a

1 Retrieve; 2 Delete; 3 Move/Rename; 4 Print; 5 Short/Long Display;
6 Look; 7 Other Directory; 8 Copy; 9 Find; N Name Search: 6
```

5. Using the arrow keys to move the cursor up, down, left, and right, highlight **CHAPTER2.LRN**.

6. Choose **1 R**etrieve by typing **1** or **R**. The CHAPTER2.LRN document appears in the typing area.

A helpful hint: Files in the List Files menu are listed in alphabetical order, making it easier for you to find a file name. Remember that the file you have retrieved is a *copy* of the original file, which remains unchanged on disk.

MOVING AROUND IN A DOCUMENT

The arrow keys help you get around in a document, but only one character or line at a time. To speed things up, other keys allow you to jump over large portions of text. These *cursor-movement* keys can take you to the end or beginning of a line, to the top or bottom of a screen, to the previous or next screen of text, to other pages in the document, and to the beginning or end of a document.

The cursor-movement keys are quite helpful, but you need not become overly concerned with memorizing them; you can always use the arrow keys. It is best to learn one or two keystrokes at a time, master them, and learn additional keystrokes as needed.

Table 2.1 lists some cursor-movement keystrokes and what they do. Keys joined by a hyphen are pressed *at the same time*. For example, while holding down the Ctrl key, press → to move to the beginning of the next word (Ctrl-→). Keys separated by a comma are used *in sequence*. For example, Home, Home, ↑ means press Home twice, and then press ↑ to move to the top of the screen.

NAVIGATING ON ONE LINE OF TEXT

Table 2.1 shows five key combinations that allow you to move the cursor back and forth on a line of text:

- Ctrl-→
- Ctrl-←
- End
- Home, →
- Home, ←

To practice moving the cursor, follow these steps at your computer:

1. Use your arrow keys to move the cursor under the *E* in *Enclosed*, in the first sentence of the first paragraph.

2. Press **Ctrl-→** *twice* to move two words to the right.

3. Press **Home,** → to move the cursor to the end of the line.

4. Press **Home,** ← to move the cursor to the beginning of the line.

5. Press **End** to move the cursor to the end of the line.

6. Press **Ctrl-←** several times until the cursor is at the left margin. The cursor moves to the left one word at a time. Pressing **Ctrl-←** again moves the cursor to the last word of the previous line.

Table 2.1   **Cursor-Movement Keys**

Keystroke	Moves the cursor:
Ctrl-→	To the beginning of the next word
Ctrl-←	To the beginning of the previous word
End	To the end of a line (scroll right)
Home, →	To the end of a line (scroll right)
Home, ←	To the beginning of a line (scroll left)
Home, ↑	To the top of the current screen
Home, ↓	To the bottom of the current screen
+ on numeric keypad	Down one screen of text
- on numeric keypad	Up one screen of text
PgDn	To the top of the next page
PgUp	To the top of the previous page
Ctrl-Home, <Page #>, Enter	To the top of the page number you typed in (using Go to)
Home, Home, ↑	To the first character on the top of page 1 (the beginning of the document)
Home, Home, ↓	To the last character of the last page (the end of the document)

 NAVIGATING THROUGH SCREENS OF TEXT

You may, at times, want to jump to a specific place in a long document. Table 2.1 shows four key combinations that allow you to move the cursor within and between screens:

- Home, ↑
- Home, ↓
- + (on the numeric keypad)

- - (on the numeric keypad)

To practice using these keys, follow these steps at your computer:

1. Press **Home, ↑**. The cursor moves to the top of the current screen.

2. Press **Home, ↓**. The cursor moves to the bottom of the screen.

3. Press **+** on the numeric keypad. The cursor moves to the next screen of text.

4. Press **-** on the numeric keypad. The cursor moves to the top of the screen.

5. Once again, press **-** on the numeric keypad. This time the cursor moves to the top of the *previous* screen.

 NAVIGATING THROUGH A DOCUMENT

Table 2.1 also shows five key combinations that allow you to move the cursor one or many pages at a time:

- PgDn

- PgUp

- Ctrl+Home, <Page #>, Enter

- Home, Home, ↓

- Home, Home, ↑

A helpful hint: Don't confuse a page with a screen! The text displayed on one screen can be more or less than one page; it is usually less.

To practice navigating, follow these steps at your computer:

1. Press **PgDn**. Examine the status line. The cursor moves to the first character of the next page. The cursor is on page 2. Your screen should look like the one shown in Figure 2.2.

2. Press **PgUp**. The cursor moves to the top of page 1. (Examine the status line to verify this.)

3. Press **Ctrl-Home**. WordPerfect prompts:

   Go to

   It is asking you what *page* you wish to go to.

Figure 2.2   **The screen after Step 1**

```
The 400 is capable of performing concurrent word processing and

data processing functions.  Compatible data file formats allow

the user to access both kinds of processing applications.  The

system will support both character and line printers and, of

course, can be augmented with telecommunication devices and other

peripherals.


Since the 400 can perform data and word processing, the

high-speed output and expandable capacity provide the advantages

of a system that will keep you current with developing

technological changes.  Our software is designed for integrated

                                          Doc 1 Pg 2 Ln 1" Pos 1"
```

4. Type **3** and press **Enter**. The cursor moves to the top of page 3.

5. Press **Home, Home,** ↓. Notice that the cursor moves to the end of the document.

6. Press **Home, Home,** ↑. The cursor moves to the top of the document. Your screen should look like the one shown in Figure 2.3.

DELETING LARGER BLOCKS OF TEXT

As you learned in Chapter 1, you can use either Backspace or Del to delete a single character. WordPerfect also has keystroke combinations that allow you to:

- Delete a word

- Delete from the cursor to the right margin

- Delete from the cursor to the end of the page

Table 2.2 lists keystroke combinations for deleting larger portions of text. Chapter 5 will show you how to highlight a block of text and then delete it.

Figure 2.3   **The screen after Step 6**

```
June 7, 1991



Mr. P. L. Jones
80 Wellington Street
Toronto, Ontario    Canada
M5K 1A2


Dear Mr. Jones:


Enclosed are two copies of your maintenance contract covering the
                                        Doc 1 Pg 1 Ln 1" Pos 1"
```

Table 2.2   **Deleting Larger Portions of Text**

Keystroke	Result
Ctrl-Backspace	Deletes the word at the cursor
Ctrl-End	Deletes from the cursor to the end of the line
Ctrl-PgDn	Deletes from the cursor to the bottom of the page

DELETING A WORD

In WordPerfect, you can delete a word using Ctrl-Backspace.

Follow these steps at your computer:

1. Move under any letter in the word *trained*, in the last sentence of the first paragraph on page 1.

2. Press **Ctrl-Backspace**. This deletes the word at the cursor, including the blank space *after* the word.

3. Press ↓. The text shifts to accommodate the deletion.

DELETING TO THE END OF THE LINE

You can also delete text from the cursor to the end of the same line. Keep in mind that *line* refers to a line on the screen: all text of the same vertical position between the left and right margins. Don't confuse a line with a sentence. A sentence usually begins with a capital letter, spans several lines, and ends with a period.

Follow these steps at your computer:

1. Move to the space between the words *you* and *within*, toward the end of the first paragraph of the letter, on page 1.

2. Press **Ctrl-End**. The text is deleted from the cursor to the right margin.

3. Type . (a period) to end the sentence after the word *you*.

DELETING TO THE END OF THE PAGE

You can also delete text from the cursor to the end of the same page.

Follow these steps at your computer:

1. Move the cursor under the *I* that begins the second paragraph.

2. Press **Ctrl-PgDn**. WordPerfect prompts

   ```
   Delete Remainder of page? No (Yes)
   ```

3. Type **Y**, and look at your screen. The text is deleted from the cursor to the bottom of the page. (If you had typed **N** you would have canceled the command.)

You may have noticed that the three deletion methods you just learned all delete text forwards (down in the document) rather than backwards (up in the document). This means that you place the cursor at the *beginning* of the portion of text that you wish to delete, not at the end.

THE UNDELETE FEATURE

Suppose you just realized that you made a mistake—you didn't mean to delete that text to the end of the page. In Chapter 1, when you issued a command, you used the Cancel key, F1, if you changed your mind. F1 can also serve as the Undelete key, and pressing it restores deleted characters. (As you use WordPerfect more, you will find that many WordPerfect commands or menus have several purposes.) The Undelete feature lets you change your mind; you can restore deleted text from the last three deletions.

A *deletion* is any character or group of characters removed by any method except the Backspace key. F1 restores text erased with Backspace unless you moved the cursor. There is no limit to the number of characters in each deletion.

There are three general steps for restoring deleted text:

- Position your cursor where you want the deleted text restored.

- Press F1.

- Choose 1 to restore the viewed text, choose 2 to view the *previous* deletion, or press F1 to cancel Restore. Press 1 after 2 to restore a deletion you just viewed.

Now follow these steps at your computer:

1. Press **F1**. Two menu choices appear on the bottom-left of your screen, and your most recent deletion (the one to the end of the page) is displayed.

2. Choose **1 R**estore. The text you deleted is now restored to the document beginning at the cursor's location.

3. Move the cursor to the beginning of the paragraph (*I have*) and press **F1**. Notice that the same text that was just restored is displayed again (the *I have* paragraph). Compare your screen to the one in Figure 2.4.

4. Choose **2 P**revious Deletion. The deletion before the last one is now displayed on the screen (from the word *within* to the end of the line).

5. Choose **2 P**revious Deletion again. The single word *trained*, which you deleted earlier, is displayed on the screen.

6. Choose **2 P**revious Deletion again. The most recent deletion is displayed (the *I have* paragraph).

7. Press **F1** to cancel the Undelete command.

A helpful hint: Position your cursor *before* pressing F1, because the text will reappear wherever the cursor is located.

Figure 2.4　　**The Undelete feature (after step 3)**

```
400 you recently purchased from us.  If you experience any

difficulty with your system, contact Harold Smith, Customer

Service.  He will have one of our service representatives call on

you.


I have also enclosed the descriptive material you requested.

Selling for $400, the 400 is a powerful stand-alone system and

represents a major advance in low-cost business computers.  Based

on the System 100, it is a multi-station configuration, capable

of handling most demanding business applications with its 256K

bytes of memory.


Undelete: 1 Restore; 2 Previous Deletion: 0
```

THE SEARCH FEATURE

Have you ever had to read through a document looking for a specific word, name, number, or series of characters? That's not a big problem if the document is a page or two long, but if it is any longer, your search could take much more time.

WordPerfect's Search feature helps you locate any series of characters or codes in your document. (You'll be learning about codes in Chapter 4.) The first step of a search is to define the *search string*, the series of characters you want WordPerfect to find. In the second step, WordPerfect automatically and quickly performs the search and shows you the results, saving you time and aggravation.

The important part of performing a search is making sure the search string *exactly* matches the text you want to find.

- If the search string consists of lowercase letters only, then Search finds occurrences of the string in both lowercase and uppercase.

- If you specify the search string as uppercase or a mix of cases, then Search finds only exact matches.

- Use spaces to distinguish words from *parts* of words. A search string, *the*, retrieves *the*, *there*, *other*, and *either*. Adding a space before and after *the* retrieves only the word *the* (capital-ized and uncapitalized).

To perform a search:

- Position the cursor at the top of the document.

- Press the Search key, F2.

- Type the string of characters you wish to find. Make sure to spell accurately and use uppercase and lowercase correctly.

- Press F2 again to start the process. If a match is found, the cur-sor jumps to the first character *past* the first match.

- To repeat the same search, press F2, verify the text (the last search string is shown), and press F2 again.

Now follow these steps at your computer:

1. Move to the top of the document (press **Home, Home,** ↑).

2. Press **F2**. As shown in Figure 2.5, WordPerfect prompts

   `-> Srch:`

Figure 2.5   **The Search prompt**

```
June 7, 1991



Mr. P. L. Jones
80 Wellington Street
Toronto, Ontario   Canada
M5K 1A2


Dear Mr. Jones:


Enclosed are two copies of your maintenance contract covering the
-> Srch:
```

3. Type **service**, your search string. Because searching for all low-ercase letters will find both uppercase and lowercase occur-rences, your search string will find *service*, *Service*, and *SERVICE*.

4. Press **F2** to begin the search. The cursor jumps to the period after *Service*.

5. Press **F2**. WordPerfect prompts

   ```
   -> Srch: service
   ```

   WordPerfect will search, by default, for the previous search string. You can press F2 to search for the next occurrence of *ser-vice*. (You could, of course, type a new search string, but for now use *service*.)

6. Press **F2** to continue the search. The second occurrence of the word is found.

7. Search for the third occurrence of *service*. When the third *ser-vice* is found, add an *s* to make the word *services*.

CHANGING THE DIRECTION OF THE SEARCH

Besides searching forward for a string (down in the document), you can also search backward (up in the document). Use Shift-F2 to search backward (from the cursor to the beginning of the docu-ment), with the cursor positioned at the bottom of the document.

THE REPLACE FEATURE

Wouldn't it be handy to be able to find a word in a document and automatically replace it with another one? For example, suppose that you just created a 30-page document with 12 references to *Consolidated Stuff, Inc.* After you finished the document, you found out that the company's name is *Amalgamated Stuff, Inc.* WordPer-fect's Replace feature allows you to search for every occurrence of *Consolidated* and replace it with *Amalgamated*, either automati-cally or case by case.

USING THE HELP FEATURE TO LEARN ABOUT REPLACE

Like the Search key, the Replace keys, Alt-F2, move the cursor to a specific set of characters or codes. They also replace them automatically with other characters or codes—or delete them by replacing them with nothing. (You will learn about codes in Chapter 4.)

You can find out more about Replace by pressing the Help key, F3. You can press F3 for Help at any time. If you press F3 for Help after activating a function (such as Replace), the Help will be *context-sensitive*—the Help screen tells you about the specific feature you are using. If you press F3 without activating a function, you can get information by following the instructions on the Help screen.

Follow these steps at your computer:

1. Move to the top of the document (**Home, Home,** ↑).

2. Press **Alt-F2**. WordPerfect prompts

   `w/Confirm? No (Yes)`

3. Press **F3**. A screen about the Replace function is displayed. Read it to find out how to use Replace and the Confirm option.

4. Press **Enter** to exit Help and return to the Replace command.

 USING REPLACE

When you use Replace, WordPerfect asks you whether you want the Confirm option on or off. With Confirm on, *you* supervise replacements, sometimes replacing, other times not. With Confirm off, replacement occurs *automatically*. Replacing with Confirm *on* is recommended, so that you control the entire process and avoid unwanted changes to your document.

When you look for text, your search string must match character for character; remember that spaces are characters too. If the search text is composed of lowercase letters only, then Replace, like Search, will find occurrences in both lowercase and uppercase. If the search text is uppercase, then Replace will find only uppercase occurrences. To find all occurrences of a word, regardless of case, you should type the replacement string as lowercase. If you were to type it as uppercase, the program would find only the uppercase occurrences of the word.

To replace text:

- Position the cursor at the top of the document.

- Press Alt-F2.

- Type Y to confirm each replacement (or N to replace automatically).

- Type the characters you wish to find and *replace*. Make sure that the spelling is exact.

- Press F2.

- Type the characters you wish to *replace with*. Make sure that the spelling is exact.

- Press F2 to start the Replace procedure. If you typed Y in Step 3, then you must type Y to make each replacement or N for no replacement. If you typed N, then all replacements will be made automatically for you.

Now follow these steps at your computer:

1. Examine the screen. As shown in Figure 2.6, WordPerfect prompts

   ```
   w/Confirm? No (Yes)
   ```

Figure 2.6　　　　**The Confirm prompt**

```
June 7, 1991



Mr. P. L. Jones
80 Wellington Street
Toronto, Ontario   Canada
M5K 1A2


Dear Mr. Jones:


Enclosed are two copies of your maintenance contract covering the
w/Confirm? No (Yes)
```

2. Type **Y**. WordPerfect prompts

```
-> Srch: service
```

The last search text is still displayed. With Confirm on, each re-placement requires your permission. If you press **N** or **Enter**, all replacements are automatic.

3. Type **400**.

4. Press **F2**. WordPerfect prompts

```
Replace with:
```

5. Type **500 Model**.

6. Press **F2**. WordPerfect prompts

```
Confirm? No (Yes)
```

7. Type **Y** to replace the first occurrence of *400* with *500 Model*. The Replace proceeds to the next occurrence, *$400*. We do not wish to change this.

8. Type **N** to leave the text intact and move to the next occurrence.

To replace from the cursor position backward (toward the beginning), follow the same steps for replacing forward, but press ↑ when you see the following prompt

```
-> Srch:
```

changing the direction of the arrow from right to left.

PRACTICE YOUR SKILLS

Continue to replace *400* with *500 Model* for the rest of the document. The prompt disappears when no other occurrences are found. The message

```
*Not found*
```

appears briefly.

 ## SAVING THE FILE WITH A NEW NAME AND EXITING

You've completed all the changes in your document. To retain the changes you've made, save the file. It's a good idea to keep your original file intact, so that you can review the skills you've learned any time you like. Saving the file under its original name would re-place it with the changed file. In this case, it is best to save the file with a new name. That way, the original file remains intact.

In WordPerfect, you can use one procedure to save the document *and* clear it from memory, instead of using two procedures, Save (Chapter 1) and Exit.

Follow these steps at your computer:

1. Press **F7**. WordPerfect prompts

   `Save document? Yes (No)`

2. Type **Y**. WordPerfect prompts

   `Document to be saved: A:\CHAPTER2.LRN`

3. Type **mychap2.lrn** and press **Enter**. WordPerfect displays the message

   `Saving C:\WP51\MYCHAP2.LRN`

   and prompts

   `Exit WP? No (Yes)`

4. Type **N** to remain in WordPerfect. Notice that the typing area is cleared.

CHAPTER SUMMARY

In this chapter, you've learned some fairly sophisticated but easy-to-use techniques for getting around a document as well as for ed-iting it.

With the Data Disk you can practice the skills that you've learned at any time. Also, try using these techniques to create and edit your own documents. If you're concerned about making mistakes in your own documents, you might want to save them under new names and work on the new files. That way you can boldly try dif-ferent techniques without being concerned about making irrevers-ible changes.

Here's a quick technique reference for Chapter 2:

Feature or Action	How to Do It
Cancel	**F1** (also Undelete)
List Files	**F5**
Retrieve a file (via List Files)	**F5**, then **1 Retrieve**
Move to beginning of next word	**Ctrl-→**
Move to beginning of previous word	**Ctrl-←**
Move to end of line (scroll right)	**End**
Move to end of line (scroll right)	**Home, →**
Move to beginning of line (scroll left)	**Home, ←**
Move to top of current screen	**Home, ↑**
Move to bottom of current screen	**Home, ↓**
Move down one screen of text	**+** on numeric keypad
Move up one screen of text	**–** on numeric keypad
Move to top of next page	**PgDn**
Move to top of previous page	**PgUp**
Move to top of page number typed in (using Goto)	**Ctrl-Home**, <Page #>, **Enter**
Move to first character in document	**Home, Home, ↑**
Move to last character in document	**Home, Home, ↓**
Delete word at position of cursor	**Ctrl-Backspace**
Delete from cursor to end of line	**Ctrl-End**
Delete from cursor to bottom of page	**Ctrl-PgDn, Y**
Undelete	**F1** (same key as Cancel)
Search (in forward direction)	**F2**
Search (in backward direction)	**Shift-F2**

Feature or Action	How to Do It
Replace	**Alt-F2, Y** (to Confirm) or **N** (for automatic Replace)
Help	**F3**

In the next chapter, you'll be learning methods for enhancing your text, such as aligning, emphasizing, and indenting. You'll also learn how to format and align text using the WordPerfect menu.

CHAPTER THREE:
TEXT ENHANCEMENT

Whether you are preparing a long report or a short letter, you can usually improve its appearance. An enhancement can be as simple as making a heading bold or right-aligning portions of text. WordPerfect provides you with many ways to enhance text, and this chapter focuses on the most important of them.

When done with this chapter, you will be able to:

- Align text
- Emphasize text, changing fonts
- Indent text
- Enhance text using the WordPerfect pull-down menus

Figure 3.1 shows the document you will produce in this chapter.

ALIGNING TEXT

Text alignment determines how text is positioned between the left and right margins. There are three kinds of text alignment: flush left, centered, and flush right. This paragraph is an example of *flush-left* alignment. The lines of text are aligned evenly along the left margin. Examples of centered and flush-right text alignment are shown in Figure 3.1.

CENTERING TEXT AS YOU TYPE

To center text on a manual typewriter, you must count the number of characters in the line of text to be centered, divide the number by two, and backspace *that* number of times from the center of the line to determine the point from which to type. On a word processor, centering, like all formatting, is a simple matter of correctly positioning the cursor and pressing one or more keys.

This is an example of centered text.
Each line of text is centered
between the left and right margins.
To center a single line,
press the Center keys,
Shift-F6,
and type the text.
To center several *single-line* paragraphs consecutively:
display the Format menu, Shift-F8,
choose 1 - Line,
3 - Justification,
and 2 - Center.

Figure 3.1   **The completed document**

```
                          Macco Plastics Inc.
                         Quarterly Sales Report
                            First Quarter

    1.    General News

            Congratulations to  all of  you!   An initial   review of the
        sales figures for the nation reveals a surge  in sales  in all of
        Macco's sales  regions.   Major new  clients have  been added and
        many new products are on the way.

            Midwestern Region

            After several years of falling sales due to the slump in the
            auto industry,  Blair Williams  and his folks have something
            to celebrate.   The recent boom in auto manufacturing has led
            to renewed demand for Macco products in Detroit.

            Northeastern Region

            Gene Davidson and his  group are doing a great job   in
            Nashua.  They have secured major  contracts for  a wide
            range  of  new  and  existing  products.   Much of this
            business is coming from  Computer Equipment Corporation
            (CEC), a major client of Macco's.

            Southern Region

            Mark Daley and his group have done a fine job of maintaining
            relations with XYZ's Product Development Division in London.
            They have been working closely with XYZ  product  people  to
            develop new products to be used  in XYZ's existing
            line.

            A companywide study will begin in March, under the direction
        of Cathy Donaldson  and  Bill  Schuster  in data  processing, to
        determine  how  to  most  effectively implement automation in our
        firm.  We will be making a large commitment to productivity gains
        via computerization sometime in the last quarter.


    2.    Conclusion

            If  the  recovery  continues  at the current pace, this year
        should be a banner year for all of us at Macco.  We want to thank
        all  of  you  for  the  outstanding  jobs  you've  done and, most
        important, for standing by Macco in hard times.  Keep up the good
        work!


        John Smith
        Regional Coordinator
        Macco Plastics, Inc.
```

If you are not already in WordPerfect, start the program as you learned in Chapter 1. If you are in WordPerfect but have text on the screen, clear the typing area. Insert your Data Disk in drive A.

Follow these steps at your computer:

1. Press **F5** to activate List Files.

2. Type **a:** and press **Enter** to display a list of the files on the Data Disk.

3. Highlight the file CHAP3A.LRN, and choose **1 R**etrieve. The file is retrieved into the typing area.

4. Move to Line 1.5", directly above the paragraph numbered *1.*, to position the cursor on a blank line.

5. Press **Shift-F6** to position the cursor at the center of the line.

6. Type **Macco Plastics Inc**. The text centers and adjusts itself as you type. Press **Enter** to end the line and return the cursor to the left margin of the next line. Each line must be centered individually.

7. Press **Shift-F6**. The cursor positions itself at the center of the line.

8. Type **Quarterly Sales Report** and press **Enter**.

If you wish to center text that you've already typed in the document, move the cursor under the first character of the line, and press Shift-F6. (Once you've pressed Shift-F6, you may have to press ↓ to adjust the changed text.)

PRACTICE YOUR SKILLS

1. Center and type the third line of the heading, **First Quarter**.

2. Press **Enter** to end the line.

ALIGNING TEXT FLUSH RIGHT

This paragraph is aligned *flush right*. Lines of text are aligned evenly along the right margin. To right-align one line of text, press the Flush-Right keys, Alt-F6, and type the text. The alignment feature shuts off automatically when you press Enter to end the line.

To right-align several *single-line* paragraphs consecutively:

• Bring up the Format menu by pressing Shift-F8.

• Choose 1 - Line.

• Choose 3 - Justification.

• Choose 3 - Right.

INSERTING THE DATE

The Date Text feature allows you to enter the current *system* date, which is supplied by your computer's built-in clock. To include *today's* date as a permanent part of the text, press the Date/Outline keys, Shift-F5, and choose Date Text (press T or 1). The Date Code option (press C or 2) adds a code to the document that inserts the *current* date whenever the document is retrieved. Date Text never changes; Date Code always reflects the current date.

RIGHT-ALIGNING THE DATE

Follow these steps at your computer:

1. Move to the top of the document (**Home, Home,** ↑).

2. Press **Alt-F6**. The cursor moves to the right margin.

3. Press **Shift-F5** to insert the date, in the format *Month dd, yyyy.*

4. Choose **1 D**ate Text. Today's date is inserted at the right margin.

5. Press **Enter** to end the line and advance the cursor to the left margin one line down.

Remember to apply flush right to each *new* line of text to be right-aligned. If you wish to right-align text that you've *already* typed in the document, move the cursor under the first character of the line, and press Alt-F6. Once you've aligned the text, you may have to press ↓ to adjust the moved text.

JUSTIFYING TEXT

Text justification determines how paragraphs with several lines are positioned between the left and right margins. Each document requires the appropriate kind of justification. Newspaper columns, for example, are typically fully justified; each line is flush with both margins.

WordPerfect has four justification settings: left, center, right, and full. Left, center, and right justification behave like left, center, and right alignment. Full justification, the default setting, produces text that is aligned evenly along both the left and right margins. (This effect may not be visible in the typing area.) In WordPerfect, justification is a kind of line formatting, available from the Line menu. (You'll learn more about line formatting in Chapter 6.)

Figure 3.2 shows a paragraph that is not fully justified. The right margin is uneven, or *ragged:* the space between words is the same from line to line. Figure 3.3 shows the same paragraph fully justified. The amount of space between words varies from line to line because the program automatically calculates the amount of space between words that is necessary to fill out, or justify, a line.

Figure 3.2   **A ragged paragraph**

```
     A companywide study will begin in March, under the direction of
     Cathy Donaldson and Bill Schuster in data processing, to
     determine how to most effectively implement automation in our
     firm. We will be making a large commitment to productivity gains
     via computerization sometime in the last quarter.
```

Figure 3.3   **The same paragraph with full justification**

```
     A companywide study will begin in March, under the direction of
     Cathy  Donaldson  and  Bill  Schuster  in  data  processing,  to
     determine  how  to  most  effectively  implement  automation in our
     firm. We will be making a large commitment to productivity gains
     via computerization sometime in the last quarter.
```

A helpful hint: To apply full justification, WordPerfect increases the space between words to justify text. Using left rather than full justification generally makes text more readable. If you do use full justification, try to hyphenate the text to reduce the irregular and sometimes large gaps between words. (You'll be learning about hyphenation in Chapter 8.)

In traditional typesetting and in some word processing and desktop publishing programs, *justification* refers only to what WordPerfect calls *full justification:* aligning text evenly along both margins. WordPerfect uses *justification* more loosely.

EMPHASIZING TEXT

One way to call attention to text is to apply text emphasis such as bold, underline, double-underline, italic, and small caps. Although WordPerfect gives you many options, try not to mix too many of them in one document. Your document will look more attractive and be more effective if you choose one or two options and use them consistently. The Font menu (Ctrl-F8), shown in Figure 3.4, enables you to change the size, appearance, base font, and, if you are using a color printer, color of text.

Figure 3.4   **The Font menu**

```
1 Size; 2 Appearance; 3 Normal; 4 Base Font; 5 Print Color: 0
```

The Appearance menu (Figure 3.5) enables you to change the text *style*. Because bold and underline are commonly used styles, they have their own separate function keys, which you will learn about later in this chapter.

UNDERLINING FROM THE FONT MENU

To underline, position your cursor and press the Font menu keys, Ctrl-F8. Choose 2 Appearance and 2 Undln, then type the text. To turn the feature off, either press → once or bring up the Appearance menu again and choose the same command you used to turn the feature on. If you choose Normal, you will cancel *all* active enhancements. If the text is already typed, you can use the Block function (which you will learn about in Chapter 5) to highlight it and choose a font effect.

Figure 3.5   **The Appearance menu**

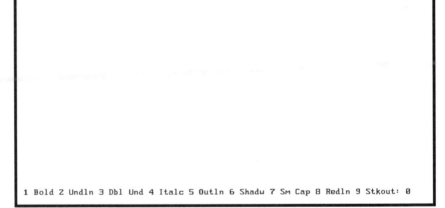

```
1 Bold 2 Undln 3 Dbl Und 4 Italc 5 Outln 6 Shadw 7 Sm Cap 8 Redln 9 Stkout: 0
```

Note: You won't be able to view some changes in text emphasis in the typing area, although they may appear as a different color if you are using a color monitor. You can examine these changes only in the View Document area (see "Using View Document" later in this chapter).

Follow these steps at your computer:

1. Move to the space after *1.* on page 1.

2. Tab to Position 1.5".

3. Press **Ctrl-F8** to display the Font menu.

4. Choose **2 A**ppearance. The Appearance menu appears at the bottom of the screen.

5. Choose **2 U**ndln to turn underlining on. (Pos confirms that underlining is on: it is underlined or a different color, depending on your monitor.)

6. Type **Introduction**. The text is underlined.

7. Press **Ctrl-F8** to display the Font menu again. Choose **2** **A**ppearance and **2** **U**ndln to turn underlining off.

8. Press **Enter** to end the line.

UNDERLINING WITH THE F8 FUNCTION KEY

Instead of using the Appearance menu to underline text, you can use the shortcut key, F8. This key is a toggle. Press F8 to turn underlining on, and type the text; turn underlining off by pressing the key again.

Follow these steps at your computer:

1. Move to the space after *2.* on page 1.

2. Tab to Position 1.5".

3. Press **F8** to turn underlining on. (Pos confirms that underlining is on: it is underlined or a different color, depending on your monitor.)

4. Type **Regional Updates**. The text is underlined.

5. Press **F8** to turn underlining off. Pos returns to normal.

6. Press **Enter** to end the line.

PRACTICE YOUR SKILLS

Go through the rest of the document, typing and underlining the following subheadings for the paragraphs numbered 3, 4, and 5:

```
Computer Study
Quarterly Meeting
Conclusion
```

Remember, underlining might not be visible on your monitor.

MAKING TEXT BOLD AS YOU TYPE

You can use the Appearance menu to apply **bold** as well as underlining. To do this, display the Font menu by pressing Ctrl-F8, choose 2 Appearance to display the Appearance menu, and choose 1 Bold.

F6 is the shortcut for applying bold. Simply press F6 and type the text. Then toggle bold off by pressing F6 once more. To apply bold to text that you've already typed, you can also use the Block feature (which you'll learn about in Chapter 5) to highlight the text, and then press F6.

Follow these steps at your computer:

1. Move the cursor under the *A* in *After several*, in the first paragraph under *2. Regional Updates*.

2. Press **Tab**.

3. Press **F6** to turn bold on. (Pos reflects that bold is active: it becomes brighter or changes color.)

4. Type **Midwestern Region**.

5. Press **F6** again to turn bold off. Pos returns to normal.

6. Press **Enter** twice to end the line and place a blank line under the subtitle.

PRACTICE YOUR SKILLS

1. Using the steps above as a guide, create the bold subtitle **Northeastern Region** for the paragraph beginning *John Martinson and his group*.

2. Create the bold subtitle **Southern Region** for the paragraph beginning *Mark Daley and his group*.

MAKING TEXT LARGER AS YOU TYPE

The first option listed in the Font menu is 1 Size (see Figure 3.4). *Size* refers to a character's height or position on a line. The Size menu, shown in Figure 3.6, enables you to format characters as subscript (H_2O) or superscript (N^2) and to select from several sizes of characters. This can be useful in texts dealing with mathematical or scientific subjects.

Follow these steps at your computer:

1. Move to the top of the document (**Home, Home, ↑**).

2. Press **Caps Lock** to turn capitalization on. The position indicator changes from Pos to POS.

Figure 3.6 **The Size menu**

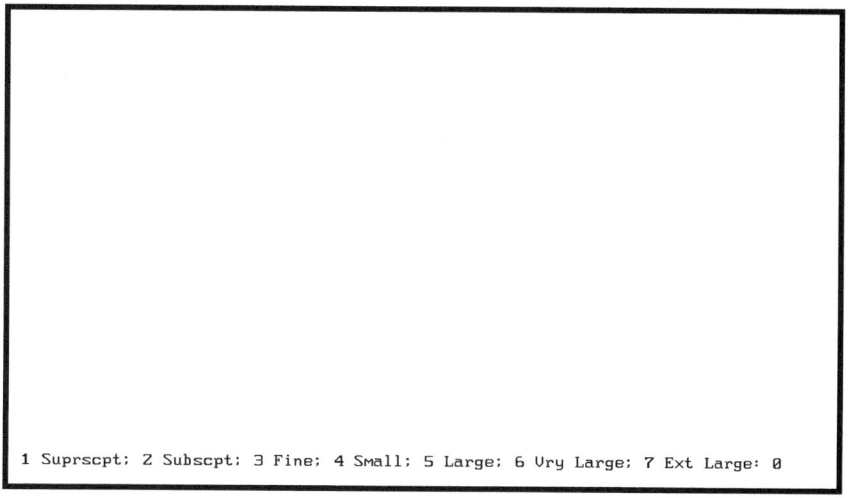

```
1 Suprscpt; 2 Subscpt; 3 Fine; 4 Small; 5 Large; 6 Vry Large; 7 Ext Large: 0
```

3. Press **Ctrl-F8**. The Font menu appears on the bottom of the screen.

4. Choose **1 S**ize. The Size menu appears on the bottom of the screen.

5. Choose **7 E**xt Large.

6. Type **INTERNAL MEMO**, the text to be formatted as extra large.

7. Press **Ctrl-F8**, choose **1 S**ize, and choose **7 E**xt Large, to restore normal fonts.

8. Press **Caps Lock** to turn capitalization off. Pos returns to normal.

9. Press **Enter** to end the line.

Like changes in appearance, changes in size cannot all be viewed in the typing area. They may, however, appear as a different color if you are using a color monitor. You can examine these size changes only in the View Document area (see "Using View Document" just ahead).

A note on printing: The way text appears when printed depends on which fonts your printer supports. If you select extra-large type, but the text is printed in the normal size, your printer probably does not offer a font larger than the one you're already using.

USING VIEW DOCUMENT

You may want to see how your changes affected your document, or you may just want to get an idea of how your document will look. The View Document feature simulates printed output on the screen. Instead of printing, press the Print keys, Shift-F7, to display the Print and Options menu (Figure 3.7), and choose 6 - View Document to view your document before printing it.

Figure 3.7   **The Print and Options menu**

```
Print

       1 - Full Document
       2 - Page
       3 - Document on Disk
       4 - Control Printer
       5 - Multiple Pages
       6 - View Document
       7 - Initialize Printer


Options

       S - Select Printer               Epson FX-80/100
       B - Binding Offset               0"
       N - Number of Copies             1
       U - Multiple Copies Generated by WordPerfect
       G - Graphics Quality             Medium
       T - Text Quality                 High




Selection: 0
```

Your document will then be shown in the *View Document* area. By default, this area shows the document in Full Page view, with either single or facing pages. You can magnify a portion of your document to 100 percent or 200 percent by choosing 1 or 2, respectively. Figure 3.8 shows the 200% view. Press F7 to leave the preview area and return to the document.

Follow these steps at your computer:

1. Press **Shift-F7** to display the Print and Options menu.

2. Choose **6 - V**iew Document from the Print menu.

3. Examine the screen. The first page of the document is in the View Document area. A menu appears at the bottom of the screen.

Figure 3.8   **The View Document area**

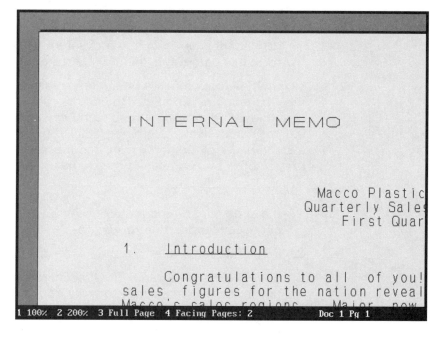

4. Choose **1 1**00%. The extra-large text is clearly visible.

5. Choose **3 F**ull Page to return to the full-page view.

6. Press **F7** to return to the typing area.

INDENTING TEXT

Indenting lines is a way of setting them off from surrounding text. In WordPerfect, *indenting* moves every line of a paragraph away from the left or right margins, or from both at the same time. Since WordPerfect lets you do this with keystrokes, you do not have to change margin settings for every paragraph you want to indent. Indentation creates a new temporary left, right, or left-right boundary, while the left and right margins remain unchanged.

COMPARING TABS AND INDENTS

Many people confuse tabs and indents. A tab indents *one* line. If you insert a tab before the first word of a paragraph, only the *first line* is indented; the other lines remain at the left margin. An indent moves the *entire paragraph* away from the left or right margin, or from both.

> Left Indent a paragraph to move it away from the left margin. As in this paragraph, left indent creates a new left boundary.

To indent before you start typing text, press F4 for Left Indent, and type the text. Pressing Enter to end the paragraph also ends the indent. Indenting must be turned on for every paragraph you wish to indent. To indent existing paragraphs, move the cursor under the first character of the paragraph, and press F4. You might have to press ↓ once or a couple of times to adjust the text.

Follow these steps at your computer:

1. Move the cursor under the *A* in *As we expected*, in the second paragraph under *1. Introduction*.

2. Press **Tab** and ↓ to adjust the text.

3. Examine the paragraph. The first character moved to the first tab stop, the first line moved away from the left margin, and the rest of the paragraph remained aligned with the left margin.

4. Move the cursor under the *A* in *After several*, under *Midwestern Region*.

5. Press **F4** to indent the paragraph.

6. Press ↓ to adjust the text to the indent. Notice the difference between the paragraph with the tab and the one with the indent. (You might have to press ↓ more than once to adjust the affected text.)

PRACTICE YOUR SKILLS

Using F4, indent the paragraph underneath the subtitle *Southern Region*. Compare your screen to the one shown in Figure 3.9.

INDENTING MORE THAN ONCE

You can indent a paragraph even farther from the left margin. To increase an indent, press F4 two or more times. The indent positions are based on tab stops. Because tab stops are set by default at every half inch, every indent moves the text one-half inch away from the margin.

Figure 3.9   **The document CHAP3A.LRN with left indents**

```
2.    Regional Updates

      Midwestern Region

      After several years of falling sales due to the slump in the
      auto industry, Blair Williams and his folks have something
      to celebrate.  The recent boom in auto manufacturing has led
      to renewed demand for Macco products in Detroit.

      Northeastern Region

John Martinson and his group are doing a great job in Nashua.
They have secured major contracts for a wide range of new and
existing products.  Much of this business is coming from Computer
Equipment Corporation (CEC), a major client of Macco's.

      Southern Region

      Mark Daley and his group have done a fine job of maintaining
      relations with XYZ's Product Development Division in London.
      They have been working closely with XYZ product people to
      develop new products to be used in XYZ's existing line.

A:\CHAP3A.LRN                              Doc 1 Pg 1 Ln 7.33" Pos 1"
```

Follow these steps at your computer:

1. Move under the letter *J* in *John Martinson*, the next paragraph, below *After several years*. (To compare different types of indents on one screen, position your cursor so that all three paragraphs are visible at once.)

2. Press **F4** twice, to indent the paragraph twice. Then press ↓ to adjust the text.

3. Examine the paragraph. It moved one inch (two tab stops) away from the left margin. Compare this paragraph to the one above.

4. Move the cursor under the *J* in *John Martinson*. Press **Backspace** twice to un-indent the text. You will be indenting it differently in the next activity.

A helpful hint: If you indent too far, you can always press Backspace to un-indent the text by deleting the Indent code. (Chapter 4 will introduce codes.)

INDENTING A PARAGRAPH FROM BOTH SIDES

Just as you can move an entire paragraph away from the left margin, you can also move it away from both the left and right margins. Left/Right Indent changes both the left and the right boundaries, as in this paragraph.

To indent before you start typing text, press Shift-F4 for Left/Right Indent, and type the text. Pressing Enter turns off indenting. Indenting must be turned on for every paragraph you wish to indent. To indent an existing paragraph, move the cursor under the first character of the paragraph, and press Shift-F4. You might have to press ↓ once or a couple of times to adjust the text.

Follow these steps at your computer:

1. Move the cursor under the *J* in *John Martinson*, if it is not already there.

2. Press **Shift-F4** to indent the paragraph from the left and right.

3. Press ↓ to adjust the text.

4. Examine the screen. Shift-F4 has increased the right as well as left margin; there's more space between the text and both margins. Compare your screen to the one shown in Figure 3.10.

You can indent more than one tab stop using Shift-F4 by pressing these keys twice or more. Keep in mind that because the paragraph is being indented from *both* sides *each* time you press Shift-F4, the lines of text can become very short. Use the Left/Right Indent with care.

 CREATING HANGING INDENTS

In a *hanging indent*, the first line of a paragraph extends to the left of the margin set for the rest of the paragraph. This paragraph has a hanging indent. This can be useful in numbered or bulleted lists in which you want the text to line up to the right of the number or bullet. Figure 3.11 shows a numbered list using hanging indents.

To produce a hanging indent for a paragraph:

• Position the cursor on the first character of the paragraph.

• Press the Left Indent key, F4, or the Left/Right Indent keys, Shift-F4.

- Press the Margin Release keys, Shift-Tab, to create a hanging indent.
- Press ↓ to adjust the text.

Figure 3.10   **Paragraph with left and right indents**

```
2.    Regional Updates

      Midwestern Region

      After several years of falling sales due to the slump in the
      auto industry, Blair Williams and his folks have something
      to celebrate.   The recent boom in auto manufacturing has led
      to renewed demand for Macco products in Detroit.

      Northeastern Region

      John Martinson and his group are doing a great job in
      Nashua.   They have secured major contracts for a wide
      range of new and existing products.   Much of this
      business is coming from Computer Equipment Corporation
      (CEC), a major client of Macco's.

      Southern Region

      Mark Daley and his group have done a fine job of maintaining
      relations with XYZ's Product Development Division in London.
      They have been working closely with XYZ product people to
      develop new products to be used in XYZ's existing line.
A:\CHAP3A.LRN                                    Doc 1 Pg 1 Ln 6.33" Pos 1"
```

Figure 3.11   **Hanging indents**

```
      The quarterly meeting will take place in Memphis this time.
You will find the agenda attached to this report.

5.    Conclusion

      The following items will be discussed at the next manager's
meeting:

1.    Marketing and sales strategies for the introduction of the
      new System 400 product line.
2.    Current available positions resulting from the early
      retirement program.
3.    Development of the new expense form to facilitate the prompt
      payment of travel reimbursements.

      If the recovery continues at the current pace, this year
should be a banner year for all of us at Macco.   We want to thank
all of you for the outstanding jobs you've done and, most
important, for standing by Macco in hard times.   Keep up the good
work!


A:\CHAP3A.LRN                                    Doc 1 Pg 2 Ln 3.83" Pos 1"
```

Tab ———

Indent ———

Follow these steps at your computer:

1. Move under the number *1* in *1. Marketing and Sales* (the first numbered paragraph on page 2, under *5. Conclusion*).

2. Press **F4** to indent the paragraph.

3. Press **Shift-Tab** to create a hanging indent. The first line of the paragraph moves to the left.

4. Press ↓ to adjust the text.

5. Examine the paragraph. It should have a hanging indent.

PRACTICE YOUR SKILLS

Using the steps above as a guide, create hanging indents for the paragraphs numbered *2* and *3* under *5. Conclusion*. Compare your screen to Figure 3.11.

SAVING THE FILE WITH A NEW NAME AND CLEARING THE TYPING AREA

Throughout this chapter, you've been making changes to the document CHAP3A.LRN, but you have not yet saved your changes. By saving the revised document as a file with a different name, you leave the original file intact and can practice your skills as often as you like.

Follow these steps at your computer:

1. Press **F7**. WordPerfect prompts

    `Save document? Yes (No)`

2. Type **Y**. WordPerfect prompts

    `Document to be Saved: A:\CHAP3A.LRN`

3. Type **MYCHAP3A.LRN** as the new file name.

4. Press **Enter**. The message

    `Saving C:\WP51\MYCHAP3A.LRN`

is displayed. The file is saved with the new name and the file name on the status line changes to C:\WP51\MYCHAP3A.LRN. WordPerfect prompts

```
Exit WP? No (Yes)
```

5. Type **N** to clear the typing area.

TEXT ENHANCEMENT AND THE WORDPERFECT MENU

Up to now, you've been using the function keys to get things done. You can usually do the same things by using WordPerfect's pull-down menus.

ACTIVATING THE PULL-DOWN MENU BAR

A *pull-down* menu consists of a list of choices extending downward from a horizontal bar, or *pull-down menu bar*, at the top of the screen. The choices are grouped into menus by functions, such as File or Graphics. The menus available on the pull-down menu bar are shown in Figure 3.12.

Figure 3.12   **The pull-down menu bar**

```
File Edit Search Layout Mark Tools Font Graphics Help        (Press F3 for Help)












                                                     Doc 1 Pg 1 Ln 1" Pos 1"
```

Press Alt-= to display the pull-down menu bar at the top of the screen. Each menu name corresponds to a pull-down menu. There are two ways to display a menu from the menu bar:

- Highlight the menu name by pressing ← or →. Press Enter to pull down the menu.

- Type the bold letter of the menu name.

Follow these steps at your computer:

1. Press **Alt-=** to display the pull-down menu bar.

2. Examine the screen. The pull-down menu bar has appeared across the top of the typing area. The File menu is highlighted.

3. Press →. On the menu bar, the cursor has advanced one menu choice to the right, and the Edit menu is highlighted.

4. Press ←. On the menu bar, the cursor has returned to File.

5. Press → until the cursor highlights **File** again. The menu is *circular,* meaning that the cursor will circle back to File. It will not fall off the edge of the menu bar and disappear.

6. Press **Enter** with the cursor highlighting **File** to pull the menu down.

7. Examine the **File** menu. All functions relate to files—creating them, saving them, renaming them, and so on.

8. Press → and examine the **Edit** menu.

9. Press **Alt-=** to remove the pull-down menu bar.

 USING PULL-DOWN MENUS

From a pulled-down menu, there are two ways to select a menu item:

- Highlight the item by using ↑ or ↓, and press Enter.

- Type its bold letter.

Menu choices with arrows next to them have submenus that appear to the *right* of the menu choice; not all menu choices have submenus. Figure 3.13 shows a typical submenu (Appearance).

To exit one menu level at a time, press F1, the Cancel key. To exit the pull-down menu bar completely, press Alt-= or F7.

Figure 3.13   **The Appearance submenu**

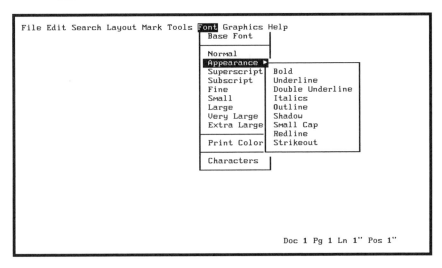

Follow these steps at your computer:

1. Press **Alt-=** to use the pull-down menu bar.

2. Highlight **Font** and press **Enter** to pull down the Font menu.

3. Press ↓ to move down one menu item, to **Normal**.

4. Press ↑ to move up one menu choice, to **Base Font**.

5. Highlight **Appearance** and press **Enter** to display and then activate the Appearance submenu.

6. Press **F1** to return to the Font menu.

7. Press **F1** again to return to the pull-down menu bar.

8. Type **F** to choose **File** from the menu bar.

9. Press **Alt-=** to remove the pull-down menu bar.

USING THE MENU TO ACTIVATE LIST FILES

In Chapter 2 you learned how to display a list of files using the List Files key, F5. You can also display a list of files using pull-down menus.

Follow these steps at your computer:

1. Press **Alt-=** to activate the pull-down menu bar.

2. Press **Enter** to pull down the File menu, the highlighted choice.

3. Use ↓ five times to highlight **List Files** and press **Enter** to activate the feature. WordPerfect prompts

   ```
   Dir C:\WP51\*.*
   ```

4. Type **a:** and press **Enter** to display a list of the files on the Data Disk.

5. Highlight and retrieve the file CHAP3B.LRN.

 ## USING THE APPEARANCE SUBMENU TO MAKE TEXT BOLD

Earlier in this chapter, you learned how to make text bold with F6. Another way is by using the Appearance submenu.

Follow these steps at your computer:

1. Move the cursor under the *M* in *Mark Daley*, underneath *2. Regional Updates*.

2. Press **Tab**.

3. Press **Alt-=** to use the pull-down menu.

4. Choose **Font** by highlighting **Font** and pressing **Enter**.

5. Choose the Appearance submenu by highlighting **Appearance** and pressing **Enter**.

6. Examine the options available from the Appearance submenu, such as Bold and Underline. The cursor is already highlighting the first item in the submenu, Bold.

7. Choose **Bold** by pressing **Enter**.

8. Examine the position indicator. It shows that bold is on; everything you type will appear in bold until it is turned off.

9. Type **Southern Region**.

10. Press **Alt-=** to activate the pull-down menu bar.

11. Choose **Font**, **Appearance**, and **B**old to turn bold off. (Choosing Font Normal would shut off *all* active size and appearance items.)

12. Press **Enter** twice to end the line and create a blank line.

A helpful hint: In Step 11 above, you could also have pressed F6 to turn bold off. If you turn a feature on using pull-down menus, you can use that feature's corresponding function key to turn it off, and vice versa. Function keys and pull-down menus offer you different ways to do the same thing.

USING THE ALIGN SUBMENU TO INDENT TEXT

You can also use the Layout menu's Align submenu to indent text.

Follow these steps at your computer:

1. Move the cursor under the letter *M* in *Mark Daley* underneath the heading *Southern Region*.

2. Activate the menu bar by pressing **Alt-=**.

3. Choose **Layout** by highlighting **Layout** and pressing **Enter**.

4. Choose **Align** by highlighting **Align** and pressing **Enter**.

5. Choose **Indent ->** to left indent the paragraph, and press ↓ to adjust the text.

6. Examine the paragraph. You can see that it is now indented. Compare your document to the one shown in Figure 3.14.

Figure 3.14   **Paragraph indented using the Align submenu**

```
2.    Regional Updates

      Midwestern Region

      After several years of falling sales due to the slump in the
      auto industry, Blair Williams and his folks have something
      to celebrate.  The recent boom in auto manufacturing has led
      to renewed demand for Macco products in Detroit.

      Northeastern Region

      John Martinson and his group are doing a great job in
      Nashua.  They have secured major contracts for a wide
      range of new and existing products.  Much of this
      business is coming from Computer Equipment Corporation
      (CEC), a major client of Macco's.

      Southern Region

      Mark Daley and his group have done a fine job of maintaining
      relations with XYZ's Product Development Division in London.
      They have been working closely with XYZ product people to
      develop new products to be used in XYZ's existing line.

A:\CHAP3B.LRN                              Doc 1 Pg 1 Ln 8.17" Pos 1"
```

USING THE MENU TO SAVE THE DOCUMENT AND CLEAR THE TYPING AREA

Earlier you learned that you can use F7 to save your document and either exit WordPerfect or clear the typing area. You can also use WordPerfect's pull-down menu to save and exit.

Follow these steps at your computer:

1. Bring up the menu bar by pressing **Alt-=**.

2. In the **File** menu, choose **Exit**. The same prompt appears—

Save document? Yes (No)

—that you get when you press F7.

3. Type **Y**. WordPerfect prompts

Document to be saved: A:\CHAP3B.LRN

4. Type **mychap3b.lrn** and press **Enter**. The message

Saving C:\WP51\MYCHAP3B.LRN

is displayed briefly. Next you see the following prompt:

Exit WP? No (Yes)

5. Type **N** to remain in WordPerfect and clear the typing area.

PRACTICE YOUR SKILLS

In the first three chapters of this book, you have learned how to create, edit, save, and print a document. You have also learned how to scroll through a document and to delete, replace, and enhance text.

The following activity gives you the opportunity to practice these skills.

This is the first such activity in this book, and there will be several others. Think of it as an opportunity to sharpen your skills. Only through repetition will you absorb what you have learned. Feel free to review the previous chapters at any time.

In this activity, you will retrieve a document from your Data Disk and then edit it to produce the final document shown in Figure 3.15.

Figure 3.15   **The corrected document**

```
                         Macco Plastics Inc.
                       Quarterly Sales Report
                          First Quarter
      1.    General News

              Congratulations to  all  of  you!   An initial  review of the
      sales figures for the nation reveals a surge  in sales  in all of
      Macco's  sales  regions.   Major new  clients have  been added and
      many new products are on the way.

              Midwestern Region

              After several years of falling sales due to the slump in the
      auto industry,  Blair Williams  and his folks have something
      to celebrate.   The recent boom in auto manufacturing has led
      to renewed demand for Macco products in Detroit.

              Northeastern Region

              Gene Davidson and his  group are doing a great job   in
      Nashua.  They have secured major  contracts for  a wide
      range  of  new  and  existing  products.   Much of this
      business is coming from  Computer Equipment Corporation
      (CEC), a major client of Macco's.

              Southern Region

              Mark Daley and his group have done a fine job of maintaining
      relations with XYZ's Product Development Division in London.
      They have been working closely with XYZ  product  people  to
      develop new products to be used  in XYZ's existing
      line.

              A companywide study will begin in March, under the direction
      of Cathy Donaldson  and  Bill  Schuster  in  data  processing, to
      determine  how  to  most  effectively implement automation in our
      firm.  We will be making a large commitment to productivity gains
      via computerization sometime in the last quarter.


      2.    Conclusion

              If  the  recovery  continues  at the current pace, this year
      should be a banner year for all of us at Macco.  We want to thank
      all  of  you  for  the  outstanding  jobs  you've  done and, most
      important, for standing by Macco in hard times.  Keep up the good
      work!


      John Smith
      Regional Coordinator
      Macco Plastics, Inc.
```

Follow these steps at your computer:

1. Clear the typing area (Chapter 1). Retrieve the file PRACTICE.CH3 (Chapter 2).

2. Search for the name *John Martinson* (Chapter 2).

3. Delete *John Martinson*. In its place type **Gene Davidson** (Chapter 1 or Chapter 2).

4. Position the cursor on the **2** near the bottom of page 1. Delete the text from the cursor to the end of the page (Chapter 2).

5. Undelete the text deleted in Step 4 (Chapter 2).

6. Move the cursor to the top of the document (Chapter 2).

7. Center the three lines at the top of the document as they appear in Figure 3.15.

8. Underline the following numbered titles:

    ```
    1. General News
    2. Conclusion
    ```

9. Use keystrokes to left indent the paragraph under the heading *Southern Region*.

10. Save the document as CORRECT.CH3 (Chapter 1).

11. Print your document (Chapter 1), and compare it to the one shown in Figure 3.15.

You may wish to enhance your skills by continuing to practice the techniques you have learned so far. If so, you can do the following activity. Refine the document you just worked on, but this time use the menu bar.

Follow these steps at your computer:

1. Clear the typing area. Use List Files to retrieve the file CHALLENG.CH3.

2. Search for *John Martinson* (Chapter 2).

3. Delete the name, and type **Gene Davidson** (Chapter 1 or Chapter 2).

4. Move the cursor to the top of the document (Chapter 2).

5. Center the heading at the top of the document, using the Align submenu.

6. Underline the following numbered titles:

    ```
    1. General News
    2. Conclusion
    ```

7. Left indent the paragraph under the heading *Southern Region*.

8. Save the document as CORRCHAL.CH3. (Use the **File** and **Save** menus.)

9. Print your document (using the **File** and **Print** menus), and compare it to the one shown in Figure 3.15.

10. Clear the typing area.

CHAPTER SUMMARY

In this chapter, you learned a number of ways to enhance your documents, including methods for aligning, emphasizing, and indenting text. With WordPerfect, you can enhance text using either function keys or pull-down menus.

Here's a quick technique reference for Chapter 3:

Feature or Action	How to Do It
Center	**Shift-F6**
List Files	**F5**
Align Flush Right	**Alt-F6**
Insert current date	**Shift-F5** (Date/Outline), **1 D**ate Text
Extra Large type	**Ctrl-F8** (Font), **1 S**ize, **7 E**xt Large
Bold	**F6**; or **Ctrl-F8** (Font), **2 A**ppearance, **1 B**old
Underline	**F8**; or **Ctrl-F8** (Font), **2 A**ppearance, **2 U**ndln
View Document	**Shift-F7** (Print), **6 - V**iew Document
100% view	**1** 100% (from View Document screen)
200% view	**2** 200% (from View Document screen)
Full-page view	**3 F**ull Page (from View Document)
Left Indent	**F4**
Left/Right Indent	**Shift-F4**
Hanging Indent	**Shift-Tab** (after indenting)
Pull-down menu bar	**Alt-=**

Remember: You've been saving your files under a new name to keep the originals unchanged. At any time, feel free to retrieve any unchanged file and go over the skills you have learned. Don't feel that you have to complete this book (or any number of chapters, for that matter) before practicing what you've learned.

In the next chapter, you'll learn about WordPerfect's formatting codes. Understanding codes will make it easier for you to edit documents and take advantage of WordPerfect's powerful formatting capabilities.

CHAPTER FOUR: CODES

Until now, you've been making a number of changes to documents. For example, you've enhanced text by underlining it or making it bold. While you've been making these enhancements, WordPerfect has been implementing them behind the scenes by inserting special codes. These codes tell your printer how to handle your changes. To print a word in bold, for example, WordPerfect inserts codes telling the printer to print bold.

When done with this chapter, you will be able to:

- Read and interpret codes
- Move around in the Reveal Codes area
- Edit and search for codes in the Reveal Codes area
- Edit codes from the typing area

THE REVEAL CODES AREA

Whenever you underline or indent text, end paragraphs, or make any changes to how your document looks, WordPerfect inserts codes. To keep the typing area clutter-free, these codes appear in the *Reveal Codes area*. WordPerfect makes it possible for you to move between the typing area and Reveal Codes area and to edit codes in either place.

 INTERPRETING CODES

Ordinarily, you need not be concerned with the Reveal Codes area when you are typing. But when you need to go back and undo formatting—underlining, for example—you must delete the code that tells the printer what and how to format. You can insert and delete codes and move around in the Reveal Codes area just as you would within the typing area.

Pressing the Reveal Codes keys, Alt-F3, displays the Reveal Codes area. With codes revealed, your screen is divided into three parts, as shown later in Figure 4.1:

Top	Text in the typing area. When you use Reveal Codes, less of the typing area can be viewed.
Tab ruler	Under the typing area's status line is the tab ruler, also known as the separator line. It shows the current margin and tab settings, where { represents the left margin, } represents the right margin, and ▲ represents a tab stop.
Bottom	Reveal Codes area. Displays the same text as the top portion of the screen, but includes the codes.

Alt-F3 is a toggle. To leave the Reveal Codes area and return to the typing area, press Alt-F3 again.

Place the Data Disk in drive A and follow these steps at your computer:

1. Retrieve the document CHAPTER4.LRN. (Press **F5**, type **a:**, and press **Enter** for the file list.) The top of the document is the part for which you would like to see codes.

2. Press **Alt-F3** to display the Reveal Codes area. Compare your screen to Figure 4.1.

Figure 4.1　　　**The Reveal Codes area**

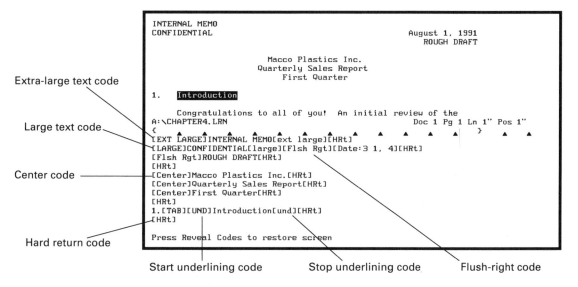

Extra-large text code

Large text code

Center code

Hard return code

Start underlining code　　　Stop underlining code　　　Flush-right code

3. Examine the three areas of the screen. Text from the top also appears in the bottom, but codes appear only in the bottom, in bold, embedded in the text. Try to identify codes for Extra Large, Center, and Flush Right.

4. Press **Alt-F3** again to return to the typing area.

MOVING AROUND IN THE REVEAL CODES AREA

Before using the Reveal Codes area, position your cursor in the part of the document whose codes you would like to see. Once you go into the Reveal Codes area, you can move the cursor just as in the typing area. As you move the cursor in the Reveal Codes area, the same text is displayed in both the top and bottom parts of the screen, with the position, line, and page indicators in the status line adjusting accordingly. Keep an eye on these indicators while you're moving around in Reveal Codes.

Follow these steps at your computer:

1. Move to the top of the document if you are not already there. This is the part of the document whose codes you will reveal.

2. Press **Alt-F3** to display the Reveal Codes area.

3. Press →. The cursor in the Reveal Codes area moves one character or code to the right, highlighting the character or code it is on. The cursor in the typing area moves in the usual way.

4. Press ↓ to move the cursor down one line.

5. Press ← to move the cursor one character or code to the left.

6. Press **Alt-F3** again to return to the typing area.

MOVING TO THE VERY TOP OF A DOCUMENT

In WordPerfect, a code affects the document from the point at which it is inserted to any code later in the document that cancels it. If, for example, the first line of text in your document is centered and you would like to precede it with a line of flush-left text, you must position the cursor *before* the code that tells WordPerfect to center text. Otherwise, a new line of text typed after the code would also be centered.

In Chapter 2, you learned to move the cursor to the beginning of the document by pressing Home, Home, ↑. But pressing Home, Home, ↑ moves the cursor only to the beginning of the *text* in the document, not to a position before any *codes* preceding the text. To move the cursor to the very top of the document (before all text and codes), press Home, Home, Home, ↑. Use these keys whenever you need to position the cursor at the very top of the document. Likewise, press Home, Home, Home, ↓, to move the cursor to the bottom of the document, beyond all text and codes.

Follow these steps at your computer:

1. Press **Alt-F3** to display the Reveal Codes area.

2. Press **Home, Home,** ↑, and examine the cursor position in the typing area. The cursor appears to be at the top of the document, on the first character of *INTERNAL MEMO*.

3. Examine the cursor position in the Reveal Codes area. The cursor is on the *I* of *INTERNAL MEMO*. The [EXT LARGE] code is *before* (to the left of) the cursor.

4. Press **Home, Home, Home,** ↑ to move the cursor to the top of the document, before all codes.

5. Examine the cursor position in the typing area. The cursor appears to be at the top of the document, on the *I* in *INTERNAL MEMO*.

6. Examine the cursor position in the Reveal Codes area. Now the cursor is highlighting the [EXT LARGE] code. This means that the cursor is truly at the top of the document.

7. Press **Alt-F3** to return to the typing area.

EDITING CODES IN REVEAL CODES

The main reason for using Reveal Codes is to remove an enhancement by deleting its code. You can also delete codes in the typing area. By deleting codes in the Reveal Codes area, you reduce the margin for error because you can see what you are doing.

DELETING CODES

Each code is treated like a single character. When the cursor is positioned on a code, the entire code is highlighted; you cannot move the cursor inside the brackets. To delete a code, highlight it with the cursor in the Reveal Codes area and press Del.

Codes for certain features are *paired*; the first code turns the feature on and the second one turns it off. For example, underlining is turned on with [UND] and off with [und]. Codes that turn a feature on are always uppercase; those that turn a feature off are always lowercase. To delete a paired code, delete only one code; its partner is deleted automatically.

Follow these steps at your computer:

1. Move under *b* in *banner year*, in the last paragraph on page 2.
2. Press **Alt-F3** to display the Reveal Codes area.
3. Position the cursor on [BOLD], the code that turns bold on. The cursor expands when it highlights [BOLD] in the bottom part of the screen.
4. Press **Del** to delete the code the cursor is on. When you delete the [BOLD] code, the [bold] code, which turns bold off, is also deleted; *banner year* is no longer bold.
5. Press **Alt-F3** to return to the typing area.

PRACTICE YOUR SKILLS

Using the steps above as a guide, remove the underline from the word *attached* (in the section titled *4. Quarterly Meeting*). Compare your screen to the one shown in Figure 4.2.

Figure 4.2 **The Reveal Codes area after completing Practice Your Skills**

```
================================================================================
4.    Quarterly Meeting

The quarterly meeting will take place in Memphis this time.  You
will find the agenda attached to this report.



5.    Conclusion

A:\CHAPTER4.LRN                                   Doc 1 Pg 2 Ln 1.5" Pos 3.1"
{    ▲    ▲    ▲    ▲    ▲    ▲    ▲    ▲    ▲    ▲    ▲    ▲    }    ▲    ▲
4.[Tab][UND]Quarterly Meeting[und][HRt]
[HRt]
The quarterly meeting will take place in Memphis this time.  You[SRt]
will find the agenda attached to this report.[HRt]
[HRt]
[HRt]
[HRt]
5.[Tab][UND]Conclusion[und][HRt]
[HRt]
The following items will be discussed at the next manager's[SRt]

Press Reveal Codes to restore screen
```

ADDING CODES

You can add text as well as codes in the Reveal Codes area. Position the cursor where you want to add text and enhancements. Then simply type and format the text as usual; your formatting changes appear as codes.

Follow these steps at your computer:

1. Move to the bottom of the document, under *Regional Coordinator*.

2. If you are not already in the Reveal Codes area, press **Alt-F3**.

3. Press **F6** to turn bold on. Both the Bold On and Bold Off codes appear in the Reveal Codes area. The cursor is on the Bold Off code.

4. Type **Macco Plastics, Inc**. The text is inserted between the Bold On and Bold Off codes.

5. Press **F6** to turn bold off. You could also have pressed → to move past the code.

6. Press **Alt-F3** to return to the typing area.

SEARCHING FOR CODES

Because the Reveal Codes area is so dense, you may find it difficult to get around. To find codes more easily, you can use WordPerfect's Search feature (F2), which you learned about in Chapter 2.

Follow these steps at your computer:

1. Move to the top of the document by pressing **Home, Home, Home,** ↑.

2. Press **F2**. WordPerfect prompts

   `-> Srch:`

3. To search for the Italic On code, press **Ctrl-F8** to display the Font menu. Choose **2 A**ppearance and **4 I**talc. Examine the Search prompt:

   `-> Srch: [ITALC]`

4. To search for the Italic On code, press **F2**, and examine the screen. The Search feature has found italic text, the word *outstanding* (see Figure 4.3).

Figure 4.3   **Italic text found using the Search feature**

```
meeting:

1.   Marketing and sales strategies for the introduction of the
     new System 400 product line.
2.   Current available positions resulting from the early
     retirement program.
3.   Development of the new expense form to facilitate the prompt
     payment of travel reimbursements.

     If the recovery continues at the current pace, this year
should be a banner year for all of us at Macco.  We want to thank
all of you for the outstanding jobs you've done and, most
important, for standing by Macco in hard times.  Keep up the good
work!


John Smith
Regional Coordinator
Macco Plastics, Inc.



A:\CHAPTER4.LRN                              Doc 1 Pg 2 Ln 4.5" Pos 1"
```

5. Press **Alt-F3** to display the Reveal Codes area.

6. Examine the Reveal Codes area. Just as in any search, the cursor is positioned directly to the right of text that matches the search string; in this case, to the right of [ITALC].

7. Highlight [ITALC] and press **Del**, or just press **Backspace**, to delete the [ITALC] code.

8. Press **Alt-F3** to return to the typing area.

DELETING CODES IN THE TYPING AREA

Although you can edit codes in the typing area, this technique can be tricky, because you must guess where the code is. Codes that indent, tab, and turn underlining on and off can be detected because the screen gives away their location. For example, if the *first* line of a paragraph is indented, there is probably a tab preceding it.

Some codes are tougher to edit. For example, the codes for a hanging indent are not paired; they consist of an Indent code and a Margin Release code, followed by a Tab code. To delete the hanging indent from the typing area, you must know when you had deleted the Indent and Margin Release codes. If you do not delete both codes, the text does not return to normal. That's why it is easier to delete codes in the Reveal Codes area.

A rule of thumb: Delete only the most obvious codes from the typing area. This will prevent you from accidentally deleting the wrong code.

The Backspace and Del keys work the same in the typing area as in the Reveal Codes area. Backspace deletes codes to the *left* of the cursor; Del deletes codes *at* the cursor. As a safeguard, when you attempt to delete certain codes from the typing area (underline, for example), WordPerfect prompts you to confirm the deletion.

Follow these steps at your computer:

1. Move the cursor to the beginning of the line that contains the word *outstanding*, in the paragraph under *5. Conclusion*. Press **Ctrl-→** until the cursor is positioned under the *o* in *outstanding*.

2. Press **Backspace**. WordPerfect prompts you for confirmation:

    ```
    Delete [UND]? No (Yes)
    ```

3. Type **Y** to delete the underline. Typing **N** would cancel the command, leaving the text intact.

4. Press **F10**. WordPerfect prompts

    ```
    Document to be saved:
    A:\CHAPTER4.LRN
    ```

5. Type **MYCHAP4.LRN**.

6. Press **Enter** to save the file as MYCHAP4.LRN. The message

    ```
    Saving C:\WP51\MYCHAP4.LRN
    ```

    is displayed.

Remember: Because it is difficult to figure out where codes are in the typing area, try to use the Reveal Codes area to delete them.

PRINTING WITH DRAFT QUALITY AND CLEARING THE TYPING AREA

If you have a printer available, you may wish to see a *hard copy* (printout) of your document at this point.

Follow these steps at your computer:

1. Press the Print keys, **Shift-F7**, to display the Print and Options menu.

2. Choose **T - T**ext Quality to change the quality of the printed text.

3. Choose **2 D**raft, for draft quality.

4. Choose **1 - F**ull Document to print the entire document. Compare your printout to the one shown in Figure 4.4.

Figure 4.4   **The completed document MYCHAP4.LRN**

```
INTERNAL MEMO
CONFIDENTIAL

                                              (Today's Date)
                                              ROUGH DRAFT

                       Macco Plastics Inc.
                       Quarterly Sales Report
                       First Quarter

    1.    Introduction

          Congratulations to  all of  you!   An initial  review of the
    sales figures for the nation reveals a surge  in sales  in all of
    Macco's sales  regions.   Major new  clients have  been added and
    many new products are on the way.

          As we expected when we entered  the field,  computer related
    products,  such as  keyboard  housings and  protective carrying
    cases, are accounting for a major portion of this upswing.

    2.    Regional Updates

          Midwestern Region

          After several years of falling sales due to the slump in the
          auto industry,  Blair Williams  and his folks have something
          to celebrate.  The recent boom in auto manufacturing has led
          to renewed demand for Macco products in Detroit.

          Northeastern Region

          John Martinson  and his  group are doing a great job in
          Nashua.  They have secured major  contracts for  a wide
          range  of  new  and  existing  products.   Much of this
          business is coming from  Computer Equipment Corporation
          (CEC), a major client of Macco's.

          Southern Region

          Mark Daley and his group have done a fine job of maintaining
          relations with XYZ's Product Development Division in London.
          They  have been working closely  with XYZ product people  to
          develop new products to be used in XYZ's existing line.

    3.    Computer Study

          A companywide study will begin in March, under the direction
    of Cathy Donaldson  and  Bill  Schuster  in  data  processing, to
    determine how  to  most  effectively implement automation in our
    firm.  We will be making a large commitment to productivity gains
    via computerization sometime in the last quarter.
```

Figure 4.4   **(continued)**

```
4.    Quarterly Meeting

The quarterly meeting will take place in Memphis this time. You
will find the agenda attached to this report.

5.    Conclusion

The following items will be discussed at the next manager's
meeting:

1.    Marketing and sales strategies for the introduction of the
      new System 400 product line.
2.    Current available positions resulting from the early
      retirement program.
3.    Development of the new expense form to facilitate the prompt
      payment of travel of travel reimbursements.

      If the recovery continues at the current pace, this year
should be a banner year for all of us at Macco. We want to thank
all of you for the outstanding jobs you've done and, most
important, for standing by Macco in hard times. Keep up the good
work!


John Smith
Regional Coordinator
Macco Plastics, Inc.
```

5. Press **F7**. WordPerfect prompts

   `Save document?  Yes (No)`

6. Type **N**. The document has already been saved; you don't have
   to save it again. WordPerfect prompts

   `Exit WP?  No (Yes)`

7. Type **N** to remain in WordPerfect but clear the typing area (and
   memory). Because *No* is the default choice, pressing Enter has
   the same effect as pressing **N**.

Looking at your printed document (or Figure 4.4), notice the bold and
underlined text, and the large font used at the top of the document.

A helpful hint: When you are printing final documents, use high-
quality print by pressing Shift-F7, T - Text Quality, and 4 High.
When you are printing drafts, choose 2 - Draft for draft quality,
which decreases the time the document takes to print.

PRACTICE YOUR SKILLS

In this chapter, you have learned skills for using the Reveal Codes area to delete codes. The following activity gives you the chance to practice what you've learned in the last few chapters. The document you will be editing contains several misplaced codes for you to find and delete (Figure 4.5).

1. Clear the typing area (Chapter 1). Retrieve the file PRACTICE.CH4 (Chapter 2).

2. Move your cursor to the first superscripted number in the document, using Figure 4.5 as a guide.

3. Find the erroneous code in the Reveal Codes area and delete it.

4. Move to the second error. Find the offending code and delete it.

5. Continue until you have corrected all ten errors.

6. Save the file as CORRECT.CH4.

7. Print the document (Chapter 1), and compare your printout to Figure 4.6.

If you have finished the above activity and would like to try another one that requires similar skills but provides a bit less guidance, try the following activity. Edit the document PRACCHAL.CH4, removing 20 erroneous codes from the typing area. Figure 4.7 shows what the document looks like with the misplaced codes. This exercise does not include any superscripted numbers to help you find the misplaced codes.

1. Clear the typing area (Chapter 1). Retrieve the file PRACCHAL.CH4 (Chapter 2).

2. Look carefully at Figure 4.7 to determine where the erroneous codes are. (Mark or number them in your book, if you wish.)

3. Move your cursor to the first item to correct. Place your cursor directly to the right or left of where you believe the code is.

4. Delete the incorrect code. Check the screen to be sure that you are deleting codes and not the text.

5. Replace any text deleted by mistake.

6. Continue until you have deleted all 20 errors.

7. Save the file as CORRCHAL.CH4 (Chapter 1).

Figure 4.5   **PRACTICE.CH4 with misplaced codes**

```
                        Macco Plastics Inc.
                       Quarterly Sales Report
                          First Quarter
     Congra    ¹tulations  to  all of  you!   An initial review of the
               sales figures   for  the  nation  reveals a surge in
               sales  in  all  of  Macco's  sales  re²gions. Major new
               clients have been  added and many   new products are
               on the way.

          As we  expected when we  entered the  field,  computer  related
     products, such  as  keyboard  housings  and protective   carrying
     cases,  are accounting for a major portion  of this upswing.

     Midwestern Re³gion

          After several years of falling sales due to the slump in the
     auto industry,  Blair Williams  and his  folks have something
     to celebrate.   The recent boom in auto manufacturing has led
     to renewed demand for Macco products in Detroit.

     Northeastern Region

          John Martinson and his group are  doing a  great job in
     Nashua.   They have secured major con    ⁴tracts   for   a
                                              wide  range  of
                                              new          and
                                              e x i s t i n g
                                              products.  Much
                                              o f    t h i s
                                              business     is
                                              coming     from
                                              C o m p u t e r
                                              Equipment
                                              Corporation
                                              (CEC),   a major
                                              client        of
                                              Macco's.

          Southern Region

          Mark Daley and his group have done a fine  job of  maintaining
     relations with  XYZ's Product  Development Division in London.
              ⁵They  have  been  worki⁶ng closely with XYZ product people
          to  develop  new  products  to be  used in XYZ's existing
          line.

          A companywide study will begin in March, under the direction
     of  Cathy Donaldson and  Bill  Schuster  in data processing, to
     determine how to most  effectively  implement  automation  in our
     firm.   We will be making a large commitment to productivity gains
     via computerization sometime in the last quarter.

          If  the  recovery  continues  at the current pace, this  year
```

Figure 4.5   **(continued)**

```
       should be a banne⁷r  year for all of us at Macco.  We want to thank
       all of  you  for   the   outstanding jobs  you've  done  and, most
       important, for standing   by Macco in hard times.  Keep up the good
       work!


       ⁸John Smith
       Reg  ⁹ional Coordinator
       Macco¹⁰ Plastics, Inc.
```

8. Print the document (Chapter 1), and compare your printout to Figure 4.6.

CHAPTER SUMMARY

In this chapter, you learned to interpret the Reveal Codes area and to move your cursor within it. You also learned how to edit codes in both the Reveal Codes area and the typing area.

Here's a quick technique reference for Chapter 4:

Feature or Action	How to Do It
Reveal Codes (On/Off)	**Alt-F3**
Very top of document	**Home, Home, Home,** ↑
Very bottom of document	**Home, Home, Home,** ↓
Print draft quality	**Shift-F7** (Print), **T** - Text Quality, **2** Draft
Print full document	**Shift-F7** (Print), **1** - Full Document

In the next chapter, you'll be learning some valuable techniques for formatting, copying, and moving blocks of text.

Figure 4.6   **Corrected PRACTICE.CH4**

```
                    Macco Plastics Inc.
                  Quarterly Sales Report
                      First Quarter

      Congratulations to all of you!  An initial review of the
   sales figures for the nation reveals a surge in sales in all of
   Macco's sales regions.  Major new clients have been added and
   many new products are on the way.

      As we expected when we entered the field, computer related
   products, such as keyboard housings and protective carrying
   cases, are accounting for a major portion of this upswing.

   Midwestern Region

   After several years of falling sales due to the slump in the
   auto industry, Blair Williams and his folks have something
   to celebrate.  The recent boom in auto manufacturing has led
   to renewed demand for Macco products in Detroit.

   Northeastern Region

   John Martinson and his group are doing a great job in
   Nashua.  They have secured major contracts for a wide
   range of new and existing products.  Much of this
   business is coming from Computer Equipment Corporation
   (CEC), a major client of Macco's.

   Southern Region

   Mark Daley and his group have done a fine job of maintaining
   relations with XYZ's Product Development Division in London.
   They have been working closely with XYZ product people to
   develop new products to be used in XYZ's existing line.

      A companywide study will begin in March, under the direction
   of Cathy Donaldson and Bill Schuster in data processing, to
   determine how to most effectively implement automation in our
   firm.  We will be making a large commitment to productivity gains
   via computerization sometime in the last quarter.

      If the recovery continues at the current pace, this year
   should be a banner year for all of us at Macco.  We want to thank
   all of you for the outstanding jobs you've done and, most
   important, for standing by Macco in hard times.  Keep up the good
   work!


   John Smith
   Regional Coordinator
   Macco Plastics, Inc.
```

Figure 4.7   **More misplaced codes (PRACCHAL.CH4)**

Macco Plastics Inc.
                                    Quarterly Sales Report
                  First Quarter

       Congratulations to all of you! An initial review of the
sales figures for the nation reveals a surge in sales in all of
                                      Macco's sales regions.
                                      Major new clients have
                                      been added and many new
                                      products are on the way.

       As we **expected when we entered the field, computer related
products, such as key**board housings and protective carrying
cases, are accounting for a major portion of this upswing.

                        Midwestern Region

       After several
years of falling sales due to the slump in the auto industry,
Blair Williams and his folks have something to celebrate. The
recent boom in auto manufacturing has led to renewed demand for
Macco products in Detroit.

       Nor theastern   Region

       John Martinson and his group are doing a great job in
Nashua. They have secured major contracts for a wide
range of new and existing products. Much of this
business is coming from Computer Equipment Corporation
(CEC), a major client of Macco's.

                                        Southern Region

Mark Daley and his group have done a fine job of maintaining
relations with XYZ's Product Development Division in London.
             They have been working closely with XYZ product
people to develop new products to be used in XYZ's existing
line.

              A companywide study will begin in March,
       under the direction of Cathy Donaldson and
       Bill Schuster in data processing, to
       determine how to most effectively implement
       automation in our firm. We will be making a
       large commitment to productivity gains via
       computerization sometime in the last quarter.

       If the recovery continues at the current pace, this year
should be a banner year for all of us at Macco. We want to thank
all of you for the outstanding jobs you've done and, most
important, for standing by   Macco in hard times. Keep up
the good work!

Figure 4.7 **(continued)**

```
John Smith
Regiona   l Coordinator

                              Macco Plastics, Inc.
```

CHAPTER FIVE:
BLOCK, MOVE,
AND SWITCH

Retrieving a
Document with
Shift-F10

Defining and
Working with
Blocks

Switching Between
Two Documents

As you write and edit, you can usually clarify your ideas by moving words around. Sometimes, moving just one word will do the trick. Sometimes, you have to move a phrase, sentence, paragraph, or even several pages to communicate as clearly as possible. When you have polished your ideas, you may want to make them stand out—to enhance them by applying bold, underline, uppercase, different letter sizes, or a combination of effects.

In this chapter, you will learn about WordPerfect's Block feature, which simplifies the process of editing and enhancing text. This feature allows you to define a block—any character or consecutive characters—and to edit, enhance, copy, and move a block as the needs of your work require. You will also learn about the Switch feature, which allows you to toggle (switch back and forth) between two open documents.

This chapter shows you how to:

- Retrieve a file by keystroke

- Define a block

- Edit and enhance blocked text

- Move and copy blocked text within a document

- Edit two documents at once

- Move and copy blocked text between documents

RETRIEVING A DOCUMENT WITH SHIFT-F10

Let's start by retrieving a document. In Chapter 2, you learned how to do this using the List Files menu (F5); you can also use the Retrieve keys, Shift-F10. To retrieve a file, you have to know the name of the document you wish to work with and type it correctly.

The typing area should be clear before you retrieve a document. If another document is present in the typing area, any document you retrieve is inserted into it. Consolidating documents can be useful (for example, in bringing together in one file the sections of a chapter). However, when you save a consolidated document, the file from which you retrieved text will *not* be saved with your changes, and you will have multiple versions of the same text.

Follow these steps at your computer:

1. Start WordPerfect and clear the typing area.

2. Press **Shift-F10** to retrieve a document. WordPerfect prompts

   `Document to be retrieved:`

3. Insert your Data Disk in drive A, type **a:\chapter5.lrn**, and press **Enter**. The document is retrieved into the typing area.

DEFINING AND WORKING WITH BLOCKS

A *block* is made up of any number of consecutive characters; you determine where the block starts and where it stops. A block can be as small as a character or as long as a document. Once you *define* a block, you can:

- Enhance it (for example, by underlining it or changing it to uppercase)

- Delete it

- Save it as a separate file

- Append it to the end of another file

- Move or copy it to another place in the same document

- Move or copy it to another place in a different document

DEFINING AND ENHANCING A BLOCK

To define a block, press the Block keys, Alt-F4, and highlight the desired text by using the arrow or cursor-movement keys. You can also take advantage of *speed highlighting:* When you type any character (letter, number, or symbol), WordPerfect highlights to the first occurrence of that character. To highlight to the end of a sentence, for example, press . (a period). If you highlight too much, use the arrow keys to remove the highlighting. To cancel the Block feature, press Alt-F4 again or the Cancel key, F1.

To enhance a block, press the appropriate function key: for example, F6 to apply bold, or F8 to underline. You can also use the pull-down menus to enhance a block.

Follow these steps at your computer:

1. Move the cursor under the *M* in *Midwestern,* under the heading *2. Regional Updates.*

2. Press **Alt-F4** to start a block. The flashing prompt

Block on

remains active until you either cancel the block (Alt-F4 or F1) or enhance it in some way.

3. Press → several times to highlight *Midwestern Region.* As you press the arrow key, each character appears in reverse video—surrounded by a bright rectangle (see Figure 5.1).

Figure 5.1   **The defined block**

```
Macco Plastics Inc.
Quarterly Sales Report
First Quarter

1.    Introduction

      Congratulations to all of you!  An initial review of the
sales figures for the nation reveals a surge in sales in all of
Macco's sales regions.  Major new clients have been added and
many new products are on the way.

      As we expected when we entered the field, computer related
products, such as keyboard housings and protective carrying
cases, are accounting for a major portion of this upswing.

      As we expected when we entered the field, computer related
products, such as keyboard housings and protective carrying
cases, are accounting for a major portion of this upswing.

2.    Regional Updates

      Midwestern Region

      After several years of falling sales due to the slump in the
Block on                                    Doc 1 Pg 1 Ln 4.5" Pos 3.2"
```

4. Press **F6** to apply bold to the highlighted text. *Midwestern Re-gion* is now bold. The highlight defining the block disappears, as does the prompt.

PRACTICE YOUR SKILLS

1. Repeat the steps above to define a block, then apply bold to the following region headings:

   Northeastern Region
   Southern Region

2. Block, then underline the following text in the numbered section headings:

   Introduction
   Regional Updates
   Computer Study
   Quarterly Meeting
   Conclusion

CENTERING A BLOCK

To center a block of text, define it, then press the Center keys, Shift-F6.

Follow these steps at your computer:

1. Move the cursor to the top of the document, before any codes, by pressing **Home, Home, Home,** ↑.

2. Press **Alt-F4** to start a block. While you are defining the block, WordPerfect prompts

   ```
   Block on
   ```

3. Press ↓ three times to highlight the three-line heading.

4. Press **Shift-F6** to center the block. The prompt

   ```
   [Just:Center?] No (Yes)
   ```

   asks you to confirm whether you want to center-justify the blocked text. *Yes* is the default.

5. Type **Y** or press **Enter**. Notice that the heading is now centered (see Figure 5.2). The highlighting disappears, as does the prompt.

Figure 5.2   **The centered heading**

```
                        Macco Plastics Inc.
                       Quarterly Sales Report
                           First Quarter

1.      Introduction

        Congratulations to all of you!  An initial review of the
sales figures for the nation reveals a surge in sales in all of
Macco's sales regions.  Major new clients have been added and
many new products are on the way.

        As we expected when we entered the field, computer related
products, such as keyboard housings and protective carrying
cases, are accounting for a major portion of this upswing.

        As we expected when we entered the field, computer related
products, such as keyboard housings and protective carrying
cases, are accounting for a major portion of this upswing.

2.      Regional Updates

        Midwestern Region

        After several years of falling sales due to the slump in the
A:\CHAPTER5.LRN                          Doc 1 Pg 1 Ln 1.5" Pos 1"
```

CHANGING THE TYPE SIZE OF A BLOCK

To change the type size of a block of text, define the block, press the Font keys, Ctrl-F8, and select 1 Size. Finally, select a size from the Size menu.

Follow these steps at your computer:

1. In the heading on the top of page 1, move the cursor under the *M* in *Macco*.

2. Press **Alt-F4** to start a block, and press ↓ three times to highlight the entire heading. Notice the flashing prompt:

   Block on

3. Press **Ctrl-F8** to display the Font menu.

4. Choose **1 S**ize, and **7 E**xt Large. Code has been added to make your text print extra large, though there may be no apparent change on your screen. The highlighting disappears, as does the prompt.

5. Press **Shift-F7** to bring up the Print menu, and choose **6 - V**iew Document to view your changes.

6. Press **F7** to return to the typing area.

CONVERTING A BLOCK TO UPPERCASE CHARACTERS

To change text to uppercase, highlight it, bring up the Switch menu by pressing Shift-F3, and select 1 Uppercase. To change a block to all lowercase, follow the same steps but select 2 Lowercase.

Follow these steps at your computer:

1. Move the cursor under the *M* in *Macco* in the heading on page 1.

2. Press **Alt-F4** to start the block. Notice the flashing prompt:

   Block on

3. Press ↓ three times to highlight the three-line heading.

4. Press **Shift-F3** to switch cases. A menu appears at the bottom of the screen, as shown in Figure 5.3.

5. Choose **1 U**ppercase. The text changes to all uppercase.

Figure 5.3 **The Switch menu**

```
                        Macco Plastics Inc.
                       Quarterly Sales Report
                          First Quarter

        1.   Introduction

             Congratulations to all of you!  An initial review of the
        sales figures for the nation reveals a surge in sales in all of
        Macco's sales regions.  Major new clients have been added and
        many new products are on the way.

             As we expected when we entered the field, computer related
        products, such as keyboard housings and protective carrying
        cases, are accounting for a major portion of this upswing.

             As we expected when we entered the field, computer related
        products, such as keyboard housings and protective carrying
        cases, are accounting for a major portion of this upswing.

        2.   Regional Updates

             Midwestern Region

             After several years of falling sales due to the slump in the
        1 Uppercase; 2 Lowercase: 0
```

Switch Menu ⎯⎯⎯⎯⎯

DELETING A BLOCK

To delete a block, highlight the text with the Block keys, press Del or Backspace, and type Y (Yes) to confirm the deletion.

Follow these steps at your computer:

1. Move to the left margin of the line beginning *As we...* in the second paragraph on page 1 (Pos 1").

2. Press **Alt-F4** to start a block. Notice the flashing prompt:

    Block on

3. Press ↓ four times to highlight the three-line paragraph *and* its trailing blank line.

4. Press **Del**. WordPerfect prompts you

    Delete Block? No (Yes)

    to confirm whether you really want to delete the block. Yes is the default.

5. Type **Y** to delete the block. (Pressing any other key would cancel the command.)

6. If necessary, press **Del** to delete any extra blank lines *before* the block.

Some helpful hints:

- The prompt

  `Delete Block? No (Yes)`

  is designed to help prevent accidental deletions. If you *do* accidentally delete something, use the Cancel/Undo key, F1, to restore, as you learned in Chapter 2.

- Sometimes, you may wish to save a block of text in a separate file. To do this, highlight the text, press F10 to save, and name the block when prompted. (The name you give the block will become its file name.)

- To copy a block of text to the end of another file, highlight the text with the Block keys and press the Move keys, Ctrl-F4. Then choose 1 Block and 4 Append, and type the name of the file to which you want to append the text.

MOVING A BLOCK OF TEXT

The Block and Move features (Alt-F4 and Ctrl-F4) make a powerful combination. To move a block of text using this combination, follow these steps:

- Use the Block keys, Alt-F4, to highlight the text you want to move.

- Press the Move keys, Ctrl-F4.

- Choose 1 Block from the Move menu.

- Choose 1 Move.

- Position the cursor at the place where you wish to move text, and press Enter.

Moving text removes it from the screen and stores it in memory; from memory it can be recalled and inserted anywhere in your document—or in several places or different documents. Even after you recall the block by pressing Enter, a copy of the block remains in memory. You can retrieve it by pressing Shift-F10 and Enter. It stays there until you move another block or until you exit WordPerfect; moving another block deletes the first moved block.

Follow these steps at your computer:

1. Move to the left margin (Position 1"), at the left of the heading *Midwestern Region* in the middle of page 1.

2. Press **Alt-F4** to start a block. WordPerfect prompts

   `Block on`

   Compare your screen with Figure 5.4.

Figure 5.4   **Preparing to highlight a block**

```
                    QUARTERLY SALES REPORT
                        FIRST QUARTER
     1.      Introduction

             Congratulations to all of you!  An initial review of the
     sales figures for the nation reveals a surge in sales in all of
     Macco's sales regions.  Major new clients have been added and
     many new products are on the way.

             As we expected when we entered the field, computer related
     products, such as keyboard housings and protective carrying
     cases, are accounting for a major portion of this upswing.

     2.      Regional Updates

             Midwestern Region

             After several years of falling sales due to the slump in the
             auto industry, Blair Williams and his folks have something
             to celebrate.   The recent boom in auto manufacturing has led
             to renewed demand for Macco products in Detroit.

             Northeastern Region
     Block on                              Doc 1 Pg 1 Ln 5" Pos 1"
```

3. Press ↓ *seven* times to block the title, the blank line, and the following paragraph.

4. Press **Ctrl-F4** to move the block. The Move menu appears at the bottom of the screen:

   `Move: 1 Block; 2 Tabular Column; 3 Rectangle: 0`

5. Choose **1 B**lock.

6. Choose **1 M**ove. The block is removed from the screen and stored in memory. You are prompted to move the cursor to the place *to which* you want to move the text:

   `Move cursor; press Enter to retrieve.`

7. Move to Position 1" of the line reading *Southern Region* and press **Enter**. The block is inserted in the new location.

It might help to think of moving and inserting text as cutting and pasting, as they are known in other programs and systems.

 COPYING A BLOCK

Copying a block of text works much the same as moving it. The *Copy* option in the Move menu places a copy of the block in memory (like Move), while the original block remains on the screen (unlike Move). Figure 5.5 shows the differences between moving and copying text. You can retrieve the copy from memory anywhere in the document or in several places, including different documents. The copy of the block remains in memory until you move or copy a different block, or until you exit WordPerfect. You can retrieve it by pressing Shift-F10 and Enter.

To copy a block:

- Use the Block keys, Alt-F4, to highlight the text you want to copy.

- Press the Move keys, Ctrl-F4.

- Choose 1 Block from the Move menu.

- Choose 2 Copy.

- Position the cursor where you wish the copy to be inserted and press Enter.

Follow these steps at your computer:

1. Move to the top of the document by pressing **Home, Home, Home,** ↑. Using Home, Home, Home, ↑ positions the cursor before the Center Justification and other codes; selecting the heading to be copied selects these codes as well. You will copy the title at the top of page 1 to the top of page 2.

2. Press **Alt-F4** to start the block. The flashing

Block on

prompt appears.

3. Block the three lines of the title *and* the trailing blank line by pressing ↓ four times.

Figure 5.5   **Moving vs. copying text**

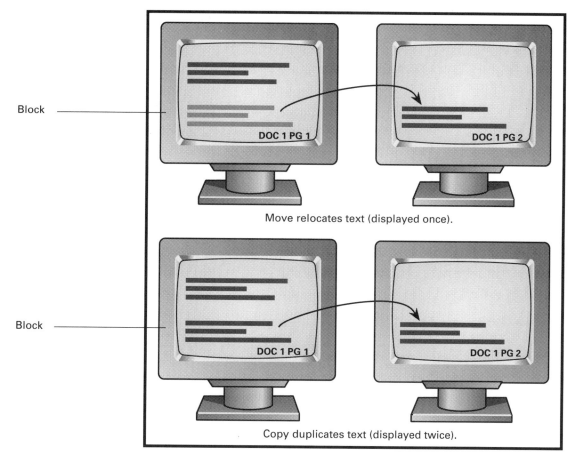

Block

Move relocates text (displayed once).

Block

Copy duplicates text (displayed twice).

4. Press **Ctrl-F4** to move the block. The Move menu appears at the bottom of the screen.

5. Choose **1 B**lock and **2 C**opy. The reverse video highlight disappears. Text remains on the screen and a copy is stored in memory. WordPerfect prompts you to specify where you want to move the block:

   `Move cursor; press Enter to retrieve.`

6. Move to the top of page 2 by pressing **PgDn**, or **Ctrl-Home** and **2** to go to page 2.

7. Press **Enter**. A copy of the block appears at the top of page 2.

8. Add or delete blank lines, if necessary.

A keyboard shortcut: After blocking text, press Ctrl-Del to move text or Ctrl-Ins to copy it; this shortcut eliminates Steps 4 and 5.

SWITCHING BETWEEN TWO DOCUMENTS

WordPerfect offers you a way to toggle between two documents. The Switch feature allows you to edit two documents in the same work session without repeatedly closing one document and retrieving the other.

Earlier you learned that when you define a block and press the Switch keys, Shift-F3, you can make the block either all uppercase or all lowercase. If you press the Switch keys with *no block defined*, the result is entirely different: You switch between *documents,* with the status line reading Doc 1 or Doc 2. This feature allows you to edit two documents at virtually the same time; it is especially handy if you want to move or copy text between documents. (See Figure 5.6.)

Figure 5.6   **The Switch Files feature**

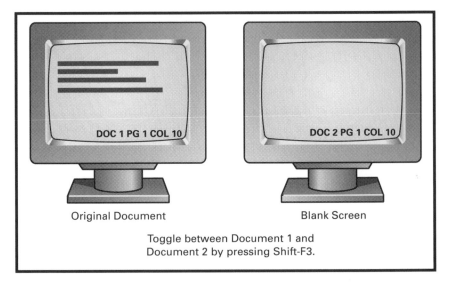

Original Document   Blank Screen

Toggle between Document 1 and
Document 2 by pressing Shift-F3.

Follow these steps at your computer:

1. Move the cursor to the top of the document by pressing **Home, Home,** ↑.

2. Press **Shift-F3** to switch documents. The status line reads:

   ```
   Doc 2 Pg 1 Ln 1" Pos 1"
   ```

   A second typing area is now available for your use. The Switch feature moves you between the two typing areas.

3. Insert the Data Disk in drive A and press **Shift-F10** to retrieve a document. WordPerfect prompts you to identify a file to retrieve:

   ```
   Document to be retrieved:
   ```

4. Type **xletter.txt** and press **Enter**. The file comes up in the typing area of Document 2.

5. Press **Shift-F3** to switch documents. The status line informs you that you are in Doc 1, editing the file CHAPTER5.LRN.

6. Press **Shift-F3** to switch documents again. The status line informs you that you are now in Doc 2, editing the file XLETTER.TXT.

7. Press **F7** to exit. WordPerfect prompts

   ```
   Save document? Yes (No)
   ```

8. Type **N** to clear the typing area without saving. (Pressing any other key would save the document.) WordPerfect prompts again, because *two* files are active:

   ```
   Exit doc 2? No (Yes)
   ```

9. Type **Y** to exit document 2 and return to document 1. (Typing N would clear the typing area and leave you in document 2.)

10. Press **F7** to exit. Again, you are prompted:

    ```
    Save document? Yes (No)
    ```

11. Type **Y**. WordPerfect prompts

    ```
    Document to be saved? A:\CHAPTER5.LRN.
    ```

12. Type **MYCHAP5.LRN** to save the document with a new name and press **Enter**. Finally, WordPerfect prompts

    ```
    Exit WP? Yes (No)
    ```

13. Type **N** to remain in WordPerfect and clear the typing area.

PRACTICE YOUR SKILLS

This section gives you the opportunity to practice the skills you just learned. You will edit a document on your Data Disk, shown in Figure 5.7, to produce the final document in Figure 5.8.

Follow these steps at your computer:

1. Clear the typing area (Chapter 1). Retrieve the file PRACTICE-.CH5.

2. Block the heading and switch to uppercase.

3. Block the heading and make it bold.

4. Block and delete the duplicate first paragraph.

5. Block the following text and make it bold:

   ```
   Northeastern Region
   Southern Region
   Midwestern Region
   ```

6. Block the paragraph title *Midwestern Region*, the blank line beneath the title, and the paragraph following the blank line. Move the block *above* the paragraph titled *Northeastern Region*.

7. Block the paragraph beginning *Congratulations,* then make it the first paragraph in the document.

8. Block and delete the duplicate paragraph beginning *If the recovery....*

9. Block and underline *banner* in the paragraph beginning with *If the recovery....*

10. Save the file as CORRECT.CH5 (Chapter 1).

11. Print the document (Chapter 1), and compare your printed version to the one shown in Figure 5.8.

If you have finished the activity, you might like to try a more challenging one requiring similar skills. Edit the document on the Data Disk, as shown in Figure 5.9, to again produce the document you just worked on, shown in Figure 5.8.

Follow these steps at your computer:

1. Clear the typing area (Chapter 1). Retrieve the file PRACOPT1-.CH5 (Chapter 2).

Figure 5.7   **The incorrect document PRACTICE.CH5**

```
                        Macco Plastics Inc.
                       Quarterly Sales Report
                          First Quarter

     As we  expected when  we entered the field, computer related
products,  such  as  keyboard  housings  and  protective carrying
cases, are accounting for a major portion of this upswing.

     As we  expected when  we entered the field, computer related
products,  such  as  keyboard  housings  and  protective carrying
cases, are accounting for a major portion of this upswing.

     Northeastern Region

     John Martinson  and his  group are doing a great job in
     Nashua.  They have secured major  contracts for  a wide
     range  of  new  and  existing  products.   Much of this
     business is  coming from Computer Equipment Corporation
     (CEC), a major client of Macco's.

     Southern Region

     Mark Daley and his group have done a fine job of maintaining
     relations with XYZ's Product Development Division in London.
     They  have been working closely  with XYZ product  people to
     develop new products to be used in XYZ's existing line.

     Midwestern Region

     After several years of falling sales due to the slump in the
     auto industry, Blair Williams  and his  folks have something
     to celebrate.  The recent boom in auto manufacturing has led
     to renewed demand for Macco products in Detroit.

     Congratulations  to all of you!  An initial  review of the
sales figures  for the nation reveals a surge in sales  in all of
Macco's sales  regions.   Major new  clients have  been added and
many new products are on the way.

     A companywide study will begin in March, under the direction
of Cathy Donaldson  and  Bill  Schuster  in data  processing, to
determine  how  to  most  effectively implement automation in our
firm.  We will be making a large commitment to productivity gains
via computerization sometime in the last quarter.

     If  the  recovery  continues  at the current pace, this year
should be a banner year for all of us at Macco.  We want to thank
all  of  you  for  the  outstanding jobs you've done and, most
important, for standing by Macco in hard times.  Keep up the good
work!

     If  the  recovery  continues  at the current pace, this year
should be a banner year for all of us at Macco.  We want to thank
all  of  you  for  the  outstanding  jobs  you've  done and, most
```

Figure 5.7   **(continued)**

```
important, for standing by Macco in hard times. Keep up the good
work!


John Smith
Regional Coordinator
Macco Plastics, Inc.
```

2. Make the last sentence of the first paragraph the first sentence of the same paragraph.

3. Move your cursor to the left margin (Pos 1") of the paragraph beginning *A companywide....*

4. Switch to the second document's typing area.

5. Retrieve the file PRACCH5.BAK *into* the second document's typing area (Chapter 2).

6. Block all three sections about regions, along with their descriptive paragraphs, and prepare to copy them into document 1.

7. Switch to document 1.

8. Retrieve the sections about regions into the document, *above* the paragraph beginning *A companywide....*

9. Block and delete the duplicate paragraph beginning *The quarterly....*

10. Move your cursor to the top of the document.

11. Switch to document 2.

12. Copy the heading. Make sure to use Home, Home, Home, ↑.

13. Switch to document 1.

14. Retrieve the heading from memory and place it at the top of the document.

15. Save the file as CORROPT1.CH5 (Chapter 1).

16. Print the document (Chapter 1), and compare it to the one shown in Figure 5.8.

17. Exit both documents.

Figure 5.8   **The corrected document**

MACCO PLASTICS INC.
QUARTERLY SALES REPORT
FIRST QUARTER

Congratulations to all of you! An initial review of the sales figures for the nation reveals a surge in sales in all of Macco's sales regions. Major new clients have been added and many new products are on the way.

As we expected when we entered the field, computer related products, such as keyboard housings and protective carrying cases, are accounting for a major portion of this upswing.

Midwestern Region

After several years of falling sales due to the slump in the auto industry, Blair Williams and his folks have something to celebrate. The recent boom in auto manufacturing has led to renewed demand for Macco products in Detroit.

Northeastern Region

John Martinson and his group are doing a great job in Nashua. They have secured major contracts for a wide range of new and existing products. Much of this business is coming from Computer Equipment Corporation (CEC), a major client of Macco's.

Southern Region

Mark Daley and his group have done a fine job of maintaining relations with XYZ's Product Development Division in London. They have been working closely with XYZ product people to develop new products to be used in XYZ's existing line.

A companywide study will begin in March, under the direction of Cathy Donaldson and Bill Schuster in data processing, to determine how to most effectively implement automation in our firm. We will be making a large commitment to productivity gains via computerization sometime in the last quarter.

If the recovery continues at the current pace, this year should be a <u>banner</u> year for all of us at Macco. We want to thank all of you for the outstanding jobs you've done and, most important, for standing by Macco in hard times. Keep up the good work!

John Smith
Regional Coordinator
Macco Plastics, Inc.

CHAPTER SUMMARY

As you have seen, the ability to work with blocks of text can help you edit your documents quickly and efficiently. This chapter has only begun to touch on the many ways you can use this powerful feature in your own work. In this chapter you've learned how to create and enhance blocks, move and copy blocks, to switch between two documents, and to copy and move blocked text between documents.

Figure 5.9   **The incorrect document PRACOPT.CH5**

An initial review of the sales figures for the nation reveals a surge in sales in all of Macco's sales regions. Major new clients have been added and many new products are on the way. Congratulations to all of you!

As we expected when we entered the field, computer related products, such as keyboard housings and protective carrying cases, are accounting for a major portion of this upswing.

A companywide study will begin in March, under the direction of Cathy Donaldson and Bill Schuster in data processing, to determine how to most effectively implement automation in our firm. We will be making a large commitment to productivity gains via computerization sometime in the last quarter.

The quarterly meeting will take place in Memphis this time. You will find the agenda attached to this report.

The quarterly meeting will take place in Memphis this time. You will find the agenda attached to this report.

If the recovery continues at the current pace, this year should be a <u>banner</u> year for all of us at Macco. We want to thank all of you for the outstanding jobs you've done and, most important, for standing by Macco in hard times. Keep up the good work!

John Smith
Regional Coordinator
Macco Plastics, Inc.

The real mastery of WordPerfect comes with practice; the more you practice the skills you've learned in this and other chapters, the more they will become second nature. You might at this point want to review any of the topics presented before moving on.

Here's a quick technique reference for Chapter 5:

Feature or Action	How to Do It
Block text	**Alt-F4**
Bold blocked text	**F6**
Underline blocked text	**F8**
Change the size or appearance of a block	**Ctrl-F8, 1 S**ize or **2 A**ppearance
Delete blocked text	**Del, Y**
Change the case of blocked text	**Shift-F3**
Save a text block as a file	**F10**, <block name>, **Enter**
Append a text block to a file	**Ctrl-F4, 1 B**lock, **4 A**ppend, <file-name> to append to, **Enter**
Retrieve a file	**Shift-F10**, <filename>, **Enter**
Switch between documents	**Shift-F3**

In the next two chapters you will learn about formatting lines and pages respectively. Together with what you know already—how to edit and enhance text, get around, work with codes, and use blocks—format skills will give you most of what you need to create your own documents.

CHAPTER SIX: LINE FORMATTING

Line Spacing

Relative Tabs

Left and Right Margins

Using the Pull-Down Menus to Format Lines

When you finish typing and editing, you should ask yourself how you can make your document look so attractive and interesting that people will want to read it. You can enhance the appearance of your document in many ways. This chapter discusses enhancements known as *line formatting;* the next chapter looks at *page* formatting.

When done with this chapter, you will be able to:

- Adjust line spacing
- Work with various types of tabs
- Change margin settings
- Use the pull-down menus to format lines

LINE SPACING

Line spacing defines the distance between lines. The default is single spacing: Every available line of the page contains text, unless a line is skipped. Text that is double-spaced wraps to every second line; triple-spaced, to every third line. Naturally, the higher the line-spacing number, the fewer the lines of text on a page. For most purposes, single or double spacing suffices.

Before you adjust line spacing, position the cursor where you want the new line spacing to begin. In WordPerfect, a change in line spacing affects the document from the position of the cursor to the bottom of the document or until another line-spacing code is encountered. You can view codes in the Reveal Codes area by pressing Alt-F3, which you learned about in Chapter 4.

To set line spacing:

- Position the cursor at the point from which you want to set line spacing.
- Press the Format keys, Shift-F8.
- Choose 1 - Line.
- Choose 6 - Line Spacing.
- Type the line-spacing value (1 for single spacing, 2 for double spacing, and so on).
- Press F7 twice to accept the change and return to the typing area.

You can also space in half-line increments (for example, 1.5"). Because not all printers support all different line spacings, consult your printer manual before fine-tuning your spacing. To reset line spacing to single spacing (the default) after using the line-spacing option, follow the steps above, typing 1 for the line-spacing value.

Follow these steps at your computer:

1. Retrieve CHAP6A.LRN from your Data Disk, using either **F5** to list files or **Shift-F10** to retrieve the file by typing its name.

2. Move to page 4 of the document by pressing **Ctrl-Home** for Goto, typing **4**, and pressing **Enter**. Examine the text. All text is single-spaced.

3. Move to the left margin of the first paragraph on page 4, which begins *The annual meeting agenda....* Figure 6.1 shows how this page will look when you're done with this chapter.

4. Press **Shift-F8** to display the Format menu.

5. Choose **1 - L**ine to display the Line menu, as shown in Figure 6.2.

6. Choose **6 - Line S**pacing, type **2** to double-space the text, and press **Enter**.

7. Press **F7** to return to the typing area.

8. Examine the text below the cursor. It should be double-spaced.

9. View the Reveal Codes area by pressing **Alt-F3**. Find the code that turns double spacing on:

   [Ln Spacing:2]

   Hide the Reveal Codes area by pressing **Alt-F3** again.

10. Press **PgUp**, and examine the screen. The line spacing on page 3 is still set to single, because space codes affect the document until the end of the document or the next space code.

11. Press **PgDn** to move the cursor to page 4.

12. Move the cursor so that it is positioned just below the first paragraph on page 4, at the left margin.

13. Press **Shift-F8** to display the Format menu.

14. Choose **1 - L**ine to display the Line menu.

15. Choose **6 - Line S**pacing, type **1** for single spacing, and press **Enter**.

16. Press **F7** to return to the typing area.

17. Examine the text below the cursor. It should be single-spaced.

Figure 6.1   **Page 4 of the completed document**

```
                        ANNUAL MEETING AGENDA

        The   annual meeting   agenda   of Macco   Plastics, Inc.

   will be held on the first   Wednesday of   the month   in the

   LLI   Amphitheatre.    The    following    items    will    be

   discussed:

        1)    The     election    of     a     corporate
              director  for   a two-year  term  to
              fill  the  vacancy  created  by  the
              resignation  of Charles E. Springon.

        2)    The  approval or  disapproval  of  a
              proposal   to acquire  a    majority
              share   of the  stock  of  Creative
              Crafts, Inc.

        The    Board   would  like    to bring  the    following

   accounts   to  the attention   of   the  stockholders.    The

   Board  Members feel  that this   information   clarifies our

   significant  gains  and supports a positive   vote   for the

   merger.

                       CREATIVE CRAFTS,  INC.

              Account      This Year     Next Year

              Taxes        $4,397.10     $4,900.71
              Loan          7,120.88      6,334.90
              Payables      8,987.55      9,786.89
```

PRACTICE YOUR SKILLS

1. Apply double spacing to the last paragraph (beginning *The Board would like...*).

Figure 6.2 **The Line menu**

```
Format: Line

      1 - Hyphenation                          No

      2 - Hyphenation Zone - Left              10%
                             Right             4%

      3 - Justification                        Full

      4 - Line Height                          Auto

      5 - Line Numbering                       No

      6 - Line Spacing                         1

      7 - Margins - Left                       1"
                    Right                      1"

      8 - Tab Set                              Rel; -1", every 0.5"

      9 - Widow/Orphan Protection              No


Selection: 0
```

2. Move to the line after the last paragraph, and restore single spacing.

RELATIVE TABS

In WordPerfect, tab stops are set by default every half inch from −1", the left edge of the paper. The different tab types offered by WordPerfect are shown in Table 6.1. These tabs can be useful in aligning text in tables of contents, creating charts and reports, and displaying numeric data.

EXAMINING THE DEFAULT TABS

You can view the default tab settings by displaying the Format menu (Shift-F8), choosing 1 - Line, and 8 - Tab Set. By default, WordPerfect uses *relative* tabs, which are set relative to the left margin setting.

Follow these steps at your computer:

1. Move the cursor below all of the text, on a line by itself.

Table 6.1   **Tab Types**

Tab Type	Aligns Text at ...
Left-aligned	First letter of word
Right-aligned	Last letter of word
Center-aligned	Center of word
Decimal	Column of numbers aligned at common character, usually a decimal point (.)
Left-aligned, with dot leader	First letter of word, preceded by a series of dots, or leader
Right-aligned, with dot leader	Last letter of word, preceded by a series of dots, or leader
Decimal, with dot leader	Columns of numbers aligned at alignment character, preceded by series of dots, or leader

2. Press **Caps Lock**, then press **Shift-F6** to center text. Type **CREATIVE CRAFTS, INC**. to title the table shown in Figure 6.1, press **Caps Lock** again, and press **Enter** twice.

3. Press **Shift-F8** to display the Format menu.

4. Choose **1 - L**ine to display the Line menu.

5. Examine the menu choice

   ```
   8 - Tab Set
   ```

   and the message

   ```
   Rel: -1", every 0.5"
   ```

   This is the default tab-stop setting, relative tab stops set every half inch beginning at −1".

6. Choose **8 - T**ab Set to activate the Tab Set area, shown in Figure 6.3.

7. Press **Home, Home**, ← to move to the left edge of the paper.

Figure 6.3   **The Tab Set area for relative tabs**

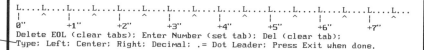

```
    1)    The election of a corporate director for a
          two-year term to fill the vacancy created by
          the resignation of Charles E. Springon.

    2)    The approval or disapproval of a proposal to
          acquire a majority share of the stock of
          Creative Crafts, Inc.

    The Board would like to bring the following accounts to the

attention of the stockholders.  The Board Members feel that this

information clarifies our significant gains and supports a

positive vote for the merger.


                        CREATIVE CRAFTS, INC.


L....L....L....L....L....L....L....L....L....L....L....L....L....L...
|    ^    |    ^    |    ^    |    ^    |    ^    |    ^    |    ^    |
0"        +1"       +2"       +3"       +4"       +5"       +6"       +7"
Delete EOL (clear tabs); Enter Number (set tab); Del (clear tab);
Type; Left; Center; Right; Decimal; .= Dot Leader; Press Exit when done.
```

Tab Set area

8. Examine the Tab Set area. The left edge of the paper is position -1". The left margin is 0". The bottom of the screen displays a line that lists the current tab settings. The numbers represent positions on the line. The *L*s represent left-aligned tabs.

In the next section you learn to reset the tab settings and use the new tabs to create a table.

CREATING CENTERED TABS FOR CENTERED COLUMN HEADINGS

Pressing the Center keys, Shift-F6, normally centers text on the line. However, if your cursor is at a center-aligned tab stop, pressing Shift-F6 centers text there. Forming columns for a table by tabbing from column to column allows you to center the column headings.

Take another look at the table shown in Figure 6.1. Before typing the table, you'll want to set tabs to center the column headings. To set centered tabs, display the Format menu by pressing Shift-F8. Choose 1 - Line and 8 - Tab Set. Find the position on the tab ruler (in the Tab Set area) where you want to set the tab, and type a lower-case or uppercase *c* (for center-aligned).

Follow these steps at your computer:

1. Press **Ctrl-End** to delete the default tab settings.

2. Position the cursor at +1" on the tab ruler (use ← and →), and type **c** or **C** to set a center-aligned tab there. Do the same at positions +3" and +4".

3. Press **F7** to leave the Tab Set area and return to the Line menu.

4. Examine the menu choice

```
8 - Tab Set
```

and the message

```
Rel: +1",+3",+4"
```

5. Press **F7** to return to the typing area.

6. Display the Reveal Codes area by pressing **Alt-F3**, and examine the code:

```
[Tab Set:Rel: +1",+3",+4"]
```

7. Hide the Reveal Codes area by pressing **Alt-F3** again.

8. Tab to the first tab stop (the first column).

9. Type **Account** (the title of the first column), and tab to the second column.

10. Type **This Year**, press **Tab**, type **Next Year**, and press **Enter** twice. Don't worry that the columns are too close together; you will fix this momentarily.

SETTING TABS FOR A TABLE

Tabs for table entries are set in much the same way as centered tabs for column headings. From the Tab Set area, press Ctrl-End to delete the existing tab settings, move the cursor to the position at which you would like to set the tab, and type the letter representing the kind of tab you would like to set.

Follow these steps at your computer:

1. Press **Shift-F8** to display the Format menu.

2. Choose **1 - Line** to display the Line menu.

3. Choose **8 - Tab Set** to use the Tab Set area.

4. Press **Home, Home,** ← to move to the left edge of the paper. Notice that the current tab settings show the last changes you made to those settings.

5. Press **Ctrl-End** to delete the tab settings.

6. Position the cursor at 1.2", and type the letter **L** to set a left-aligned tab there.

7. Position the cursor at 3.2", and type **d** or **D** to set a decimal tab there. Do the same at position 4.7".

8. Press **F7** twice to return to the typing area.

TYPING A TABLE

Once you've made your settings, tab to each stop, and type the text.

Follow these steps at your computer:

1. Tab to the first stop (the first column of the table).

2. Type **Taxes**. The left-aligned relative tab aligns the *T* in *Taxes* at position 1.2". Press **Tab**. WordPerfect prompts

    Align char = .

    until you type a decimal point.

3. Type **$4,397.10**. The prompt disappears when you type the dot (.) after the **7**.

4. Press **Tab**.

5. Type **$4,900.71** and press **Enter**.

PRACTICE YOUR SKILLS

Finish entering the table as shown in Figure 6.4. You will improve the apearance of this table in later activities.

MOVING CENTER-ALIGNED TAB SETTINGS

If you don't like the position of a tab stop, move it to another location. From the Tab Set area, position the cursor under the tab you wish to move, and press Ctrl-→ or Ctrl-← to move it to the right or left.

Follow these steps at your computer:

1. Move to position 1" on the line that contains the column headings.

2. Display the Reveal Codes area by pressing **Alt - F3**. Position the cursor past the Tab Set code, if necessary, and hide the Reveal Codes area by pressing **Alt - F3** again.

Figure 6.4   **The completed table with relative tabs**

```
    2)    The approval or disapproval of a
          proposal to acquire a majority
          share of the stock of Creative
          Crafts, Inc.

      The Board would like to bring the following

    accounts to the attention of the stockholders.  The

    Board Members feel that this information clarifies our

    significant gains and supports a positive vote for the

    merger.


                CREATIVE CRAFTS, INC.

            Account        This Year        Next Year

            Taxes          $4,397.10        $4,900.71
            Loans           7,120.88         6,334.90
            Payables        8,987.55         9,786.89

A:\CHAP6A.LRN                           Doc 1 Pg 4 Ln 7.67" Pos 1.5"
```

3. Press **Shift-F8** to display the Format menu.

4. Choose **1 - Line** to display the Line menu.

5. Choose **8 - T**ab Set to use the Tab Set area.

6. Position the cursor on the centered tab at 1".

7. Use **Ctrl-→** to position the tab stop at 1.5".

8. Examine the screen. The column heading *Account* is centered over the column.

9. Position the cursor on the centered tab stop at 4", the third tab stop.

10. Use **Ctrl-→** to position the tab stop at 4.5".

11. Press **F7** twice to return to the typing area. Compare page 4 of your document with Figure 6.1.

DELETING THE OLD TAB SET CODE

You now have *two* consecutive Tab Set codes in the typing area. Remember to remove unnecessary codes from your documents, so that they do not interfere with formatting. As you learned in Chapter 4, if you delete codes from the Reveal Codes area, you can see what you're doing and won't accidentally delete the wrong code.

Follow these steps at your computer:

1. Display the Reveal Codes area by pressing **Alt-F3**, and observe the new Tab Set code. There are now two Tab Set codes for the centered headings.

2. Press ← twice to position the cursor on the old code:

   ```
   Tab Set:Rel +1,+3,+4
   ```

3. Press **Del**.

4. Hide the Reveal Codes area by pressing **Alt-F3**.

 RESTORING DEFAULT TABS

Now that you are done typing the table, you should reset the tabs to the default settings. Otherwise, the tabs you set for the table will remain in effect for the rest of the document.

Follow these steps at your computer:

1. Move the cursor to a position just below the table, on a line by itself.

2. Press **Shift-F8** to display the Format menu.

3. Choose **1 - L**ine to display the Line menu.

4. Choose **8 - T**ab Set to use the Tab Set area.

5. Move to the *L* at Position 1.2", and press **Del** to delete the tab stop at the cursor.

6. Press **Home, Home,** ←, and press **Ctrl-End** to delete all the tab stops from the cursor to the right margin.

7. Type **-1,.5** and press **Enter**. This places left-aligned tabs every half inch, starting from position -1", the left edge of the paper. This is the default tab setting for every document.

8. Press **F7** to exit the Tab Set area and return to the Line menu.

9. Examine the menu choice:

   ```
   8 - Tab Set
   ```

   The message

   ```
   Rel: -1", every 0.5"
   ```

   shows that the tabs are set back to the default setting.

10. Press **F7** to return to the typing area.

A helpful hint: The method you just used to reset tabs to the default setting can also be used to set them at regular intervals. Remember to delete existing tabs before setting new ones.

LEFT AND RIGHT MARGINS

Margins define the length of the line on which text appears on screen and in print. The left and right margins are measured in inches from the left and right edges of the paper, respectively. If you are using 8.5" x 11" paper and the margins are 1 inch each, then 6.5 inches remain for text on each line.

New left and right margins are set from the cursor position forward (down) in your document. If you wish to change margin settings for the entire document, press Home, Home, ↑ to position the cursor at the top of the document (after any codes). To type half inches when setting margins, use a decimal. For example, for margins of an inch and a half, type 1.5.

Follow these steps at your computer:

1. Move to the top of page 4 using ↑ or Goto.

2. Press **Shift-F8** to display the Format menu.

3. Choose **1 - L**ine to display the Line menu.

4. Choose **7 - M**argins. WordPerfect prompts you to set the left margin.

5. Type **1.5** and press **Enter** to set a left margin of 1.5 inches.

6. Type **1.5** for the right margin as well, and press **Enter**.

7. Press **F7** to return to the typing area.

8. Display the Reveal Codes area by pressing **Alt-F3**. WordPerfect displays your selection:

`[L/R Mar:1.5",1.5"]`

9. Hide the Reveal Codes area by pressing **Alt-F3** again.

10. Press ↑ several times to move to the word *enclosure* at the bottom of page 3.

11. Examine the new margins. Because the left margin of page 3 is 1", text appears farther to the left than the text on page 4, which now has a left margin of 1.5".

12. Save the document as MYCHAP6A.LRN, and clear the typing area.

USING THE PULL-DOWN MENUS TO FORMAT LINES

You can format lines with WordPerfect's pull-down menus, which you learned about in Chapter 3. This gives you another way to adjust margins and line spacing, which can be helpful if you forget keystrokes or if you use a mouse.

USING MENUS TO CHANGE MARGINS

To change left and right margin settings using the pull-down menus, bring up the menu bar by pressing Alt-=. Choose Layout and Line to display the Line submenu, as shown in Figure 6.2. Choose 7 - Margins, and set each margin by typing a number. For fractions of an inch, type decimals. Press F7 to accept the changes and close the menu.

Follow these steps at your computer:

1. Retrieve the file CHAP6B.LRN. The document is similar to CHAP6A.LRN.

2. Bring up the WordPerfect menu bar by pressing **Alt-=**.

3. Choose **Layout** and **Line** to display the Line submenu.

4. Choose **7 - M**argins, and set both margins to 1.5".

5. Press **F7** to return to the typing area.

6. The document looks the same. Scroll down page 1 using ↓, and examine the screen. The text adjusts to the new margin settings as you scroll.

USING MENUS TO CHANGE LINE SPACING

You can also use WordPerfect's pull-down menus to change line spacing. With the menu bar displayed, choose Layout and Line to bring up the Line submenu. Then choose 6 Line Spacing. Type in a number to set the line spacing you would like, press Enter, and press F7 to accept the change and leave the typing area.

Follow these steps at your computer:

1. Move the cursor to the top of the document, under the *1* in *1. Introduction*.

2. Activate the menu by pressing **Alt-=**.

3. Choose **Layout** and **Line** to display the Line submenu.

4. Choose **6 - Line Spacing**, type **1.5** to set line spacing at an inch and a half, and press **Enter**.

5. Press **F7** to accept the change and return to the typing area.

6. Rename the document by saving it as MYCHAP6B.LRN, and clear the typing area.

PRACTICE YOUR SKILLS

In this chapter you have learned several ways to make your work look better. The next activity gives you the opportunity to practice formatting lines. The instructions guide you through the creation of the document shown in Figure 6.5.

1. Clear the typing area (Chapter 1).

2. Retrieve the file PRACTICE.CH6.

3. Complete the chart in Figure 6.5. Use the decimal tabs already set to align the numbers in the columns.

4. Change the line spacing to 2.

5. Type the last paragraph, as shown in Figure 6.5, beginning with *Those stockholders* and ending with *meeting*.

6. Rename the document CORRECT.CH6 (Chapter 1).

7. Print your work (Chapter 1).

8. Compare your printout to Figure 6.5.

If you have finished this activity and want to try one that is a bit more challenging, follow the instructions below. Use the document in Figure 6.6 as a model.

1. Clear the typing area and retrieve the document PRACOPT1-.CH6.

2. Move to the bottom of the document.

3. Change the line spacing to 1.

Figure 6.5   **Using decimal tabs**

```
                      ANNUAL MEETING AGENDA


        The annual  meeting of Macco Plastics, Inc. will be

held on the  first  Wednesday of the month,  in  the LLI

Amphitheater. The purpose of the meeting shall be:

        The  election  of  a  corporate director for a
        two-year term to fill  the vacancy  created by
        the resignation of Charles E. Springon.

                The  approval  or  disapproval  of a
                proposal  to  acquire  a  majority
                share  of  the  stock  of Creative
                Crafts, Inc.

        The  Board  would  like  to  bring  the  following

accounts  to  the  attention  of  the stockholders.  The

Board Members feel that  this information  clarifies our

significant gains  and supports  a positive vote for the

merger.

            Account      This Year      Next Year

        Taxes. . . . . . . .$3,296.09. . . $3,899.60
        Loans Payable. . . . 1,538.44. . . . .899.75
        Accounts Payable . . 4,140.54. . . .5,688.38
        Benefits . . . . . . 3,600.00. . . .5,450.00
        Deferred Income. . . 387.90. . . . .476.25

        Those stockholders  of record  at the  close of the

business day, are entitled to  receive  this  notice and

to vote at the stated meeting.
```

4. Erase all tabs. Set center-aligned tabs at positions 2.0", 3.5", and 5.0".

5. Type the column headings *1st Year*, *2nd Year*, and *3rd Year* at positions 2.0", 3.5", and 5.0", respectively.

6. Erase all tabs. Set a left-aligned tab at position .3". Set decimal tabs with dot leaders at positions 2.1", 3.6", and 5.1". For dot-leader tabs, type the alignment letter and then a period.

7. Complete the table on the second page of Figure 6.6.

8. Reset the tabs to every half inch, beginning at position 1.5".

9. Restore double spacing.

10. Type the remainder of the document, beginning with *The Board* and ending with *vote*.

11. Rename the document CORROPT1.CH6 (Chapter 1).

12. Print the document (Chapter 1).

13. Compare your printout to Figure 6.6.

CHAPTER SUMMARY

In this chapter, you've learned about line formatting with Word-Perfect: how to set different kinds of tabs, adjust intervals, and create tables using tabs. You've also learned how to set left and right margins and to change line formatting options using Word-Perfect's pull-down menus.

Here's a quick technique reference for Chapter 6:

Feature or Action	How to Do It
Change line spacing	**Shift-F8** (Format), **1 - Line**, **6 - Line Spacing**, then type number
Change margin settings	**Shift-F8** (Format), **1 - Line**, **7 - Margins**
Set tabs	**Shift-F8** (Format), **1 - Line**, **8 - Tab Set**

The next chapter introduces techniques for gaining even more control over the look of your work. You'll learn about page formatting—page length, page breaks, and headers and footers. These and other techniques define the page as a whole. Effective use of line and page formatting techniques can make all your documents more attractive.

Figure 6.6   **The completed document (CORROPT1.CH6)**

```
                        ANNUAL MEETING AGENDA


        The annual  meeting of Macco Plastics, Inc. will be

    held on the first  Wednesday  of the month,  in  the LLI

    Amphitheater. The purpose of the meeting shall be:

        The  election  of  a  corporate director for a
        two-year term to fill  the vacancy  created by
        the resignation of Charles E. Springon.

            The  approval  or  disapproval  of a
            proposal   to  acquire   a   majority
            share  of  the  stock  of  Creative
            Crafts, Inc.

        The  Board  would  like  to  bring  the  following

    accounts  to  the  attention  of  the stockholders.  The

    Board Members feel that  this information  clarifies our

    significant gains  and supports  a positive vote for the

    merger.

            Account      This Year        Next Year

        Taxes. . . . . . $3,296.09. . . .$3,899.60
        Loans Payable. . .1,538.44. . . . . 899.75
        Accounts Payable . .4,140.54. . . . 5,688.38
        Benefits . . . . .3,600.00. . . . 5,450.00
        Deferred Income. . .387.90. . . . . 476.25

        Those stockholders  of record  at the  close of the

    business  day,  are entitled to  receive this notice and

    to vote at the stated meeting.
```

Figure 6.6   **(continued)**

Additional information follows about the proposed
merger company.   Creative Crafts, Inc. was established
in May, 1985, by two men: Joshua Miller and Peter
Stevens.   They shared a common interest in crafts,
especially quilting. Over the years, their company has
grown to 29 employees, and their sales revenues have
steadily increased to $786,000 per year. The chart
below reflects the growth in some of their major
products.

                    1st Year   2nd Year   3rd Year

```
Yarn  . .$25,000.00. .$57,000.00. . . $93,000.00
Cloth . . 10,000.00. . 15,000.00 . . . 23,900.00
Quilting. 30,000.00. . 50,000.00 . . .102,000.00
```

The Board hopes that this information proves
valuable as you consider the merger.   For further
information, or to answer any questions, please call
Anna Scott, the Public Relations director at Creative
Crafts, Inc.

Please be present at the annual meeting to cast
your vote.

CHAPTER SEVEN:
PAGE FORMATTING

Pagination

Page Formatting
Options

You face some new challenges as your documents get longer. Perhaps you want to keep related sections of text together on one page. Perhaps you want to center several lines of a title vertically on a page. Perhaps you want to number pages. These effects are all achieved by *page formatting*.

In Chapter 6, you learned techniques for controlling the appearance of lines. In this chapter, you'll learn to control the appearance of the overall page. When done with this chapter, you will be able to:

- Insert and delete manual page breaks
- Center text vertically on the page
- Create headers and footers
- Number pages

PAGINATION

Pagination means dividing text into pages, separated by discrete page breaks and usually numbered sequentially. In WordPerfect, there are two kinds of page breaks, automatic and manual.

AUTOMATIC (SOFT) PAGE BREAKS

When you type enough lines of text to fill a page, WordPerfect automatically inserts a page break. An *automatic* page break is inserted by the program itself, and is known as a soft page break. The soft page break shows up on the screen as a row of dashes (---) that extends from the left margin to the right margin.

With your Data Disk in drive A, follow these steps at your computer:

1. Retrieve the document A:\CHAPTER7.LRN.

2. View the document by pressing **Shift-F7** and choosing **6 - V**iew Document. The document is three pages long, with the second page containing only two lines.

3. Press **PgDn** to see more of the document.

4. Exit to the typing area by pressing **F7**.

5. Move to the top of the document.

6. Press the **+** key on the numeric keypad three times to advance three screens of text.

7. Move the cursor under the *3* in *3. Computer Study*. Notice that an automatic page break splits the paragraph, as shown in Figure 7.1. The automatic page break appears as a row of single dashes, the manual page break between pages 2 and 3 as a row of equal signs.

Figure 7.1   **Automatic and manual page breaks**

Automatic page
break

Manual page
break

```
3.    Computer Study

        A companywide study will begin in March, under the direction
of Cathy Donaldson and Bill Schuster in data processing, to
determine how to most effectively implement automation in our
-----------------------------------------------------------------------
firm.  We will be making a large commitment to productivity gains
via computerization sometime in the last quarter.

=======================================================================
4.    Quarterly Meeting

        The quarterly meeting will take place in Memphis this time.
You will find the agenda attached to this report.

5.    Conclusion

        The following items will be discussed at the next manager's
meeting:

1.    Marketing and sales strategies for the introduction of the
A:\CHAPTER7.LRN                                    Doc 1 Pg 1 Ln 9.17" Pos 1"
```

8. Display the Reveal Codes area by pressing **Alt-F3**. The Soft Page code [SPg] in the middle of the paragraph, following the word *firm,* cannot be deleted.

9. Hide the Reveal Codes area and return to the typing area by pressing **Alt-F3**.

MANUAL (HARD) PAGE BREAKS

By inserting automatic page breaks, WordPerfect saves you the trouble of deciding where to break each page. However, there are times when you must specify where you want a page to begin or end. For example, it's common practice to begin each section of a document (particularly if the section begins with a heading) on a new page, even if the program would not automatically break the page there.

A manual, or *hard,* page break is used to break a page where *you* wish; it is a way of overriding WordPerfect. A manual page break necessarily occurs before the page would break automatically; you cannot force WordPerfect to exceed a specific number of text lines per page. In the typing area, a manual page break appears as a row of equal signs (double-dashed line). Figure 7.1 shows a manual page break.

Deleting a Manual Page Break

To delete a manual page break in the typing area, position your cursor directly above the page break and press Del. Alternatively, move your cursor below the page break and press Backspace. To delete a manual page break from the Reveal Codes area, press Backspace with the cursor to the *right* of the code or Del with the cursor *on* the code.

Follow these steps at your computer:

1. Move your cursor to the *4* in *4. Quarterly*, on page 3. The row of equal signs (double-dashed line) on your screen represents the manual, or hard, page break.

2. Display the Reveal Codes area by pressing **Alt-F3**. Notice the Hard Page Break code [HPg], as shown in Figure 7.2.

Figure 7.2   **Page breaks and Hard Page Break code**

Hard Page Break code

```
        A companywide study will begin in March, under the direction
of Cathy Donaldson and Bill Schuster in data processing, to
determine how to most effectively implement automation in our
--------------------------------------------------------------------------
firm.  We will be making a large commitment to productivity gains
via computerization sometime in the last quarter.


========================================================================
4.   Quarterly Meeting
A:\CHAPTER7.LRN                                    Doc 1 Pg 3 Ln 1" Pos 1"
{         ^    ^    ^        ^         ^     ^    ^   ^   }    ^     ^
via computerization sometime in the last quarter.[HRt]
[HRt]
[HPg]
4.[TAB][UND]Quarterly Meeting[und][HRt]
[HRt]
[Tab]The quarterly meeting will take place in Memphis this time. [SRt]
You will find the agenda attached to this report.[HRt]
[HRt]
[HRt]
5.[TAB][UND]Conclusion[und][HRt]

Press Reveal Codes to restore screen
```

3. Position the cursor on [HPg].

4. Press **Del** to delete the code.

5. Hide the Reveal Codes area and return to the typing area by pressing **Alt-F3**. The manual page break should be gone.

Inserting a Manual Page Break

To insert a manual page break as you are typing, press Ctrl-Enter at the point where you would like the page to break. The double-dashed line appears, the cursor advances to the new page, and the page number in the status line increases by one. If you'd like to insert a manual page break after typing text, position the cursor *under* the first character that you want to appear on the new page, and press Ctrl-Enter.

Follow these steps at your computer:

1. Move the cursor under the *3* in *3. Computer Study* (at the bottom of page 1).

2. Press **Ctrl-Enter** to insert a page break. Notice the row of equal signs (double-dashed line) marking the end of the page. The manual page break is placed above the cursor. The parts of the section beginning *3. Computer Study* appear together on one page, and the automatic page break has disappeared. Your manual page has fewer lines than WordPerfect's automatic page.

3. Move the cursor to the top of the document, and position it under the *1* in *1. Introduction*.

4. Press **Ctrl-Enter** to insert a page break, and examine the screen. The title is now on a separate page.

5. Display the document in the View Document area by pressing **Shift-F7** and choosing **6 - V**iew Document. The document now has three pages, the title page plus two report pages. The title is at the top of page 1.

6. Exit to the typing area by pressing **F7**.

7. Save the document as MYCHAP7.LRN. Use **F10** to save, but continue working.

PAGE FORMATTING OPTIONS

WordPerfect's Page menu controls the appearance and amount of text on a page. In the upcoming sections, you will learn three very important page formatting techniques:

- Centering text vertically on the page

- Adding headers and footers

- Numbering pages

To display the Page menu, press the Format keys, Shift-F8, and choose 2 - Page.

CENTERING TEXT VERTICALLY

Charts, tables, and brief letters are examples of short pages that may require special treatment. In such cases, you might want to center the text vertically, equally distant from the top and bottom margins.

To center text vertically on a page:

- Position the cursor at the top of the page.
- Select the Page menu (Shift-F8, 2 - Page).
- Choose 1 - Center Page (top to bottom) to center the page vertically.
- Type Y (Yes) to confirm.
- Press F7 to return to the typing area.

Follow these steps at your computer:

1. Move the cursor to the top of the document, if necessary.
2. Display the **Format** menu by pressing **Shift-F8**.
3. Choose 2 - **P**age to display the Page menu.
4. Choose 1 - **C**enter Page (top to bottom).
5. Type **Y** to confirm.
6. Press **F7** to return to the typing area.
7. Go to the Reveal Codes area by pressing **Alt-F3**, and find the code [Center Pg].
8. Press **Alt-F3** again to return to the typing area.
9. View the document by pressing **Shift-F7** and choosing **6 - V**iew Document. The title is now centered vertically on page 1, as shown in Figure 7.3.
10. Return to the typing area by pressing **F7**.

Figure 7.3   **The centered title**

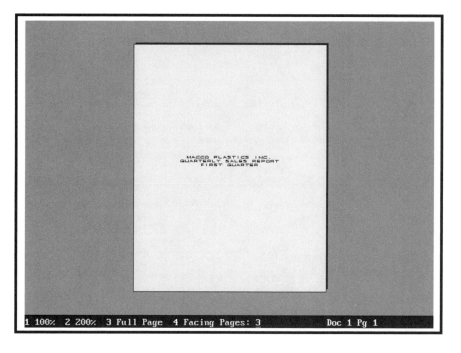

 CREATING A HEADER

In longer documents, you may wish to include a *header,* repeating text at the top of every page: a date, chapter title, section heading, department name, or some combination of these items, for example. You can create up to two different headers per document. You would use a second header if you were planning to print a two-sided bound document and wanted different (alternating) headers on left and right pages. A header is created in its own mini-document area, and it can be as long as one page. Of course, a header longer than a few lines begins to limit the space for regular text.

Most of WordPerfect's enhancement features work within headers. For example, you can create a header with text that is centered, flush right, bold, or underlined. You can also insert the date by using the Date function, Shift-F5.

To create a header:

- Position the cursor at the top of the first page on which you want the header to appear.

- Press the Format keys, Shift-F8.

- Choose 2 - Page.

- Choose 3 - Headers.

- Choose 1 Header A or 2 Header B. (Choose Header B only if you are creating the second of two headers for alternating pages.)

- Choose 2 Every Page, 3 Odd Pages, or 4 Even Pages to specify the pages on which to print the header you are creating.

- Type the text that you want the header to contain.

- Press F7 to exit to the Page menu.

- Press F7 again to return to the typing area.

To discontinue a header, move your cursor to the beginning of the appropriate page; follow the steps above, but instead of typing in header text, choose Discontinue from the Header/Footer menu. To delete a header altogether, delete the header code in the Reveal Codes area.

Follow these steps at your computer:

1. Move the cursor to the top of page 2. (The title page of most documnets does not contain a header.) Use Goto by pressing **Ctrl-Home**, typing a page number, and pressing **Enter**.

2. Display the Format menu by pressing **Shift-F8**.

3. Choose **2** - **P**age to display the Page menu.

4. Choose **3** - **H**eaders.

5. Choose **1** Header **A**.

6. Choose **2** Every **P**age to tell WordPerfect to display the header on every page of the document.

7. Press **Shift-F5** to display the Date menu, and choose **1** Date **T**ext.

8. Press **Enter** twice to end the current line and leave a blank line.

9. Press **F7** to leave the header area and return to the Page menu. At menu choice 3 - Headers, notice the message:

`HA Every page`

10. Press **F7** to return to the typing area.

Remember: When you add a header, change line spacing, or adjust margins, you limit the amount of text that can appear on a page. Because the header does not print in the top margin but in the *active* part of the page, it must share this area with regular text. Word-Perfect automatically adjusts the pagination of the document, according to line spacing, margin settings, and any headers or footers.

 CREATING A FOOTER

WordPerfect also lets you create footers, repeated text at the bottom of every page. You can create up to two different footers per document. You would use a second footer if you were planning to print a two-sided bound document and wanted different (alternating) footers on left and right pages.

Like a header, a footer is created in its own mini-document area, and it can be as long as one page. Most of WordPerfect's enhancement features work within footers. For example, you can create a footer with text that is centered, flush right, bold, or underlined. You can also use the Date function, Shift-F5, within a footer.

To create a footer:

- Position the cursor at the top of the first page on which you want the footer to appear.

- Press the Format keys, Shift-F8.

- Choose 2 - Page.

- Choose 4 - Footers.

- Choose 1 Footer A or 2 Footer B. (Choose Footer B only if you are creating the second of two footers for alternating pages.)

- Choose 2 Every Page, 3 Odd Pages, or 4 Even Pages to specify the pages on which to print the footer you are creating.

- Type the text that you want the footer to contain.

- Press F7 to exit to the Format Page menu.

- Press F7 again to return to the typing area.

To discontinue a footer from the current page forward, move your cursor to the beginning of the appropriate page, follow the steps above, but instead of typing in footer text, choose Discontinue from the Header/Footer menu. To delete a footer altogether, delete the footer code in the Reveal Codes area.

INCLUDING PAGE NUMBERS IN A HEADER OR FOOTER

To automatically number pages in a header or footer, position your cursor where you want the page number to appear within the header or footer, and press Ctrl-B. The symbol ^B appears. Pages will be numbered sequentially, beginning with page 1. As you make changes that will affect spacing and margins, WordPerfect automatically updates page numbers. To make the page numbering appear as *Page <#>* with *<#>* representing the actual page number, create a footer, align the cursor (flush left, center, or flush right), type *Page,* press the spacebar to add a space after *Page,* and press Ctrl-B. The footer now reads *Page ^B.*

Follow these steps at your computer:

1. Make sure the cursor is positioned at the top of page 2. If necessary, use Goto by pressing **Ctrl-Home**, typing **2**, and pressing **Enter**.

2. Display the **Page** menu, if necessary.

3. Choose **4 - Footers**.

4. Choose **1** Footer **A**.

5. Choose **2** Every **Page**.

6. Press **Alt-F6** to right-align the text. The footer text will appear in the bottom-right corner of the page.

7. Type **Page** to create the footer text, then press **Spacebar, Ctrl-B,** and **Enter** twice. The screen displays

   Page ^B

   The ^B tells WordPerfect to insert the page number automatically.

8. Press **F7** to leave the footer area and return to the Page menu. At the menu choice 4 - Footers, notice the message:

   FA Every page

9. Press **F7** to return to the typing area.

10. Press **Alt-F3** to examine the header and footer codes:

```
[Header A:Every page;(today's date)[HRt][HRt]
[Footer A:Every page;[Flsh Rgt]Page ^B[HRt][HRt]
```

11. Press **Alt-F3** again to return to the typing area.

Remember that adding a footer reduces the amount of text that can appear on a page.

 ## VIEWING AND PRINTING THE FINAL DOCUMENT

Now that you've formatted the pages of your document in various ways, let's look at the results. In this procedure, you will open your document in the View Document area and, if you are satisfied, print it.

Follow these steps at your computer:

1. Display the View Document area, and examine the document. Headers, footers, page numbering, and text can all be seen at the same time, giving you an idea of what the printout will look like.

2. Return to the typing area.

3. Save the document using **F10**, and type **Y** at the Replace prompt.

4. Press **Shift-F7**.

5. Choose **1 - F**ull Document to print the entire document. Compare your printout to the one shown in Figure 7.4.

6. Save the document and clear the typing area.

CHAPTER SUMMARY

In this chapter, you have learned several important page formatting techniques, such as paginating manually, centering text vertically, and creating headers and footers.

Here's a quick technique reference for Chapter 7:

Feature or Action	How to Do It
Manual page break	**Ctrl-Enter**
Center page vertically	**Shift-F8** (Format), **2 - P**age, **1 - C**enter Page (top to bottom), **Y**
Header	**Shift-F8** (Format), **2 - P**age, **3 - H**eaders, **1** Header **A** or **2** Header **B**, **2** Every **P**age
Footer	**Shift-F8** (Format), **2 - P**age, **4 - F**ooters, **1** Footer **A** or **2** Footer **B**, **2** Every **P**age

In the next chapter, you'll learn how you can use WordPerfect to correct spelling and improve the clarity and accuracy of your text.

Figure 7.4   **The final document MYCHAP7.LRN**

```
                    MACCO PLASTICS INC.
                  QUARTERLY SALES REPORT
                      FIRST QUARTER
```

Figure 7.4   **(continued)**

```
(Today's Date)


1.   Introduction

     Congratulations to  all of  you!   An initial  review of the
sales figures for the nation reveals a surge  in sales  in all of
Macco's sales  regions.   Major new  clients have  been added and
many new products are on the way.

     As we expected when we entered  the field,  computer related
products,  such as  keyboard housings  and  protective carrying
cases, are accounting for a major portion of this upswing.

2.   Regional Updates

     Southern Region

     Mark Daley and his group have done a fine job of maintaining
     relations with XYZ's Product Development Division in London.
     They have been working  closely  with  XYZ product people to
     develop new products to be used in XYZ's existing line.

     Northeastern Region

     John Martinson and his group are  doing a  great job in
     Nashua.   They have  secured major contracts for a wide
     range of new  and  existing  products.    Much  of this
     business is  coming from Computer Equipment Corporation
     (CEC), a major client of Macco's.

     Midwestern Region

     After several years of falling sales due to the slump in the
     auto industry,  Blair Williams  and his folks have something
     to celebrate.  The recent boom in auto manufacturing has led
     to renewed demand for Macco products in Detroit.

     Southern Region

     Mark Daley and his group have done a fine job of maintaining
     relations with XYZ's Product Development Division in London.
     They  have  been  working closely with XYZ product people to
     develop new products to be used  in XYZ's existing line.

                                                          Page 2
```

Figure 7.4   **(continued)**

(Today's Date)

3.   Computer Study

       A companywide study will begin in March, under the direction
of Cathy Donaldson and Bill Schuster in data processing, to
determine how to most effectively implement automation in our
firm. We will be making a large commitment to productivity gains
via computerization sometime in the last quarter.

4.   Quarterly Meeting

       The quarterly meeting will take place in Memphis this time.
You will find the agenda attached to this report.

5.   Conclusion

       The following items will be discussed at the next manager's
meeting:

1.   Marketing and sales strategies for the introduction of the
       new System 400 product line.
2.   Current available positions resulting from the early
       retirement program.
3.   Development of the new expense form to facilitate the prompt
       payment of travel reimbursements.

       If the recovery continues at the current pace, this year
should be a banner year for all of us at Macco. We want to thank
all of you for the outstanding jobs you've done and, most
important, for standing by Macco in hard times. Keep up the good
work!

John Smith
Regional Coordinator
Macco Plastics, Inc.

Page 3

Figure 7.4   **(continued)**

```
(Today's Date)

                    ANNUAL MEETING AGENDA

     The  annual  meeting  agenda  of Macco  Plastics,  Inc.

will be held on  the first  Wednesday of  the month  in  the

LLI  Amphitheatre.       The     following    items    will    be

discussed:

     1)   The     election     of     a     corporate
          director    for    a  two-year  term  to
          fill  the  vacancy    created  by    the
          resignation  of  Charles  E.  Springon.

     2)   The  approval  or   disapproval  of  a
          proposal    to    acquire    a    majority
          share   of   the   stock   of  Creative
          Crafts, Inc.

     The   Board   would  like   to  bring   the   following

accounts  to  the  attention  of  the   stockholders.    The

Board  Members  feel  that this  information  clarifies  our

significant  gains  and  supports a positive  vote  for  the

merger.

                    CREATIVE CRAFTS, INC.

          Account      This Year      Next Year

          Taxes        $4,397.10      $4,900.71
          Loan          7,120.88       6,334.90
          Payables      8,987.55       9,786.89

                                            Page 4
```

CHAPTER EIGHT:
THE SPELLER,
HYPHENATION, AND
THE THESAURUS

The WordPerfect
Speller

Hyphenation

The WordPerfect
Thesaurus

In previous chapters, you've learned how to create, edit, and enhance a document. After you complete a draft, you probably want to review it carefully, checking for errors in spelling and grammar. You may also want to make sure that you've used words correctly and expressed yourself as clearly as possible. WordPerfect's Speller and Thesaurus enable you to do these tasks more efficiently and accurately.

In this chapter, you'll learn how to use these features to correct and clarify your writing. You'll also learn how to use hyphenation to improve the spacing of fully justified text and to make left-aligned and right-aligned text less ragged. When done with this chapter, you will be able to:

- Use the Speller

- Hyphenate text

- Use the Thesaurus

THE WORDPERFECT SPELLER

The Speller helps you proofread a document by searching for each word in a list of correctly spelled words—a 100,000-word dictionary! Any misspelled word can be either replaced with a word from a list of possible corrections or edited to alter its spelling. You can spell-check a word, a block, a page, or your entire document. After every spell-check, the Speller tells you the number of words checked.

The Speller also features *pattern lookup* and *phonetic lookup*. Using pattern lookup, you type those letters of a word that you know, substituting *wildcards* for the letters you don't know. Word-Perfect then lists possible matching words from which you can select a word to place in your document. In *phonetic lookup*, the Speller looks up homonyms: words that sound like the incorrectly spelled word. These homonyms are listed on the screen, and you can select one to replace the incorrect word.

Many documents contain properly spelled words that are not in the Speller dictionary, such as proper names and acronyms. You can instruct the Speller to continue the spell-check without correcting these words. You can even add words that the Speller dictionary does not have (for example, company names) to a *supplemental dictionary*. When you use those words in future documents, they will be considered correct. WordPerfect also checks for the occurrence of repeated words (*the the*, for example) and words containing both letters and numbers.

CHECKING AN ENTIRE DOCUMENT FOR SPELLING

To use the Speller to check spelling for an entire document:

- Save the document.

- Position the cursor at the top of the document.

- Press the Spell keys, Ctrl-F2.

- Choose 3 Document.

- When the Speller highlights a misspelled word, use the menu in the Spell area (in the lower half of the screen) to make any corrections, and continue.

- When the spell-check is complete, press any key to return to the typing area.

- Save the document.

Follow these steps at your computer:

1. Retrieve CHAPTER8.LRN from your Data Disk.

2. Press the Spell keys, **Ctrl-F2**, to bring up the Speller.

3. Choose **3 D**ocument. WordPerfect spell-checks the document, stopping at the first word it cannot find in its dictionary, *Macco*—a company name. WordPerfect prompts

   `Word not found`

4. Examine the split screen, as shown in Figure 8.1. The typing area is displayed in the upper half of the screen, with *Macco* highlighted. The bottom half of the screen, the Speller area, displays a list of alternative words and a menu.

5. Choose **2 Skip**. Because *Macco* is a proper name and is correctly spelled, you are instructing WordPerfect to skip this and every occurrence of the name for the rest of the document. (To skip *Macco* in this document *and* add it to the supplemental dictionary used to spell-check other documents, you would press 3 Add.) The Speller then moves on to the next word not found, *Fiancial*. A list of alternatives appears on the screen. (In this case, WordPerfect provided only one possible correction.) Choose a word from the list by typing the corresponding letter.

6. Type **A** to insert *Financial* in the text.

Figure 8.1   **The WordPerfect Speller**

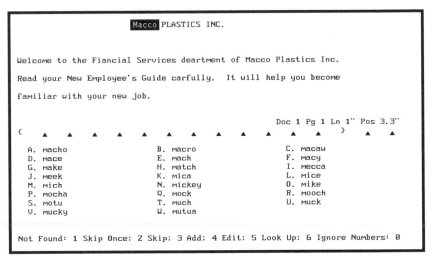

PRACTICE YOUR SKILLS

Continue hunting and correcting misspelled words until you find *clinete*. Stop here for now; you'll be continuing in the next activity.

LOOKING UP THE SPELLING OF A WORD

You can also use the Speller to check the spelling of an individual word while you are typing.

- Position the cursor anywhere within the word you want to check.

- Press the Spell keys, Ctrl-F2.

- Choose 1 Word.

- Make the correction, if necessary.

Follow these steps at your computer:

1. The misspelled word *clinete* should be highlighted (from the last "Practice Your Skills" section). The intended word was *clientele*, but *clientele* is not on the list of suggested words in the Speller area. To find the correct word, you must use a wildcard.

2. Choose **5** Look Up. You see the prompt

   Word or Word Pattern:

3. Type **client*** and press **Enter**. The asterisk (*) is the wildcard character, which tells WordPerfect to list all words beginning with *client* and ending with any number of letters (for example, *clients* and *clientele*). The new word list in the Speller area includes *clientele*, choice C.

4. Type **C** to replace *clinete* with the correctly spelled word *clientele*.

PRACTICE YOUR SKILLS

1. Continue correcting the misspelled words.

2. When you complete the spell-check, press **F7** to return to the typing area.

HYPHENATION

Text that is left-justified has a ragged-right margin, and text that is right-justified has a ragged-left margin. To maintain the ragged margin but reduce raggedness, you can hyphenate the text. Fully justified text has smooth margins but gappy spacing between words. To fill in the gaps and improve the text fit, you can, again, hyphenate the text.

To hyphenate a document:

- Position the cursor at the top of the document.

- Display the Line menu by pressing Shift-F8, 1 - Line, choosing 1 Hyphenation, and setting it to Yes.

- Press F7 to return to the document.

WordPerfect uses special dictionary files when hyphenating your documents. The program asks you to manually hyphenate a word only when the hyphenation program cannot find a word in its dictionary files: for example, a company name, proper name, or foreign expression. Look at the hyphenated document shown in Figure 8.2.

To cancel hyphenation for a particular word, position the cursor on the first character of the hyphenated word and press the Home key together with a forward slash (Home-/). Then, delete the hyphen character. The whole word wraps to the next line. If you turn hyphenation on or off, a code is automatically inserted in the document. Like a line-spacing or margin code, a hyphenation code affects the document from its position forward. If you want to hyphenate the entire document, simply move to the top of the document before turning on hyphenation.

Figure 8.2   **A hyphenated document**

```
the United States and Canada.  All facilities include convenient-
ly located customer service centers--only minutes away from
convention sites, city attractions, and public transportation.

While Macco's clientele consists primarily of manufacturers, we
also supply some items to retail outlets.  In both arenas, our
reputation is for providing high quality products and reliable
services.  We are prod to have you join this tradition.


Read the organization chart on the facing page.  It will show you
just where your department lies in the chain of command.  It will
also help you become acquainted with the names and responsibili-
A:\CHAPTER8.LRN                               Doc 1 Pg 1 Ln 7.33" Pos 1"
```

To turn off hyphenation from the position of the cursor forward, display the Line menu by pressing Shift-F8, 1 - Line, choosing 1 Hyphenation, and typing N. When you turn off hyphenation, existing hyphens are not affected; you must manually delete the hyphens in portions of the document no longer governed by automatic hyphenation.

If you edit your text or change paragraph indents, type, type size, or printer drivers, the text shifts. If hyphenation has been turned on for a document, it is automatically rehyphenated; if a long word is no longer hyphenated, the hyphen is no longer visible on the screen.

WordPerfect has several hyphenation characters that allow you to control the division of words, especially long words or words that need to be kept together.

• Use a normal hyphen (-) to break the word at the end of a line.

- Use a *nonbreaking* or *hard* hyphen (Home, hyphen) for hyphenated words, such as *Mrs. Jayne Smith-Howe*, that should not be broken at the end of a line.

- The *soft hyphen* appears automatically when words are broken into syllables at the end of a line.

- Press Home, -, - to keep two hyphens together, forming a dash.

Follow these steps at your computer:

1. Move the cursor to the top of the document.

2. Display the **Line** menu by pressing **Shift-F8** and **1 - Line**.

3. Choose **1** Hyphenation, and type **Y** (Yes) to turn on hyphenation.

4. Press **F7** to accept the change and return to the document.

5. Observe your document, scrolling down to look at the result of turning on hyphenation. Compare your screen to the one shown in Figure 8.2.

THE WORDPERFECT THESAURUS

If you can't find the exact word you would like to use and want to look up a group of words with similar meanings, you can use WordPerfect's on-line Thesaurus to find *synonyms* (words or phrases with similar meanings). The Thesaurus also provides you with *antonyms* (words or phrases with opposite meanings).

When you press the Thesaurus keys, Alt-F1, the Thesaurus area appears in the lower part of the screen. This area has three columns, as shown in Figure 8.3. The *headword*, the word you are looking up, appears at the top of the first column. Word *references* appear underneath the head word. References are divided into as many as four *subgroups* underneath the headword: nouns, verbs, adjectives, and antonyms. Not all headwords have all four subgroups.

The references in the first column have letters next to them, allowing you to replace the word you have looked up with a lettered reference. To replace the headword with a word appearing in the second or third column, press → to go to the column. The column with the cursor contains the lettered references.

To look up synonyms and antonyms for a word in your document:

- Position the cursor on the word you want to look up.

Figure 8.3   **The WordPerfect Thesaurus**

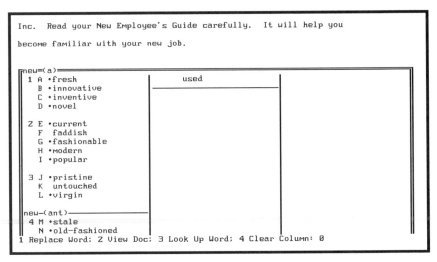

- Press the Thesaurus keys, Alt-F1.

- Position the cursor in the column that contains the word you want by pressing ← or →.

- Choose 1 Replace Word, and type the bold letter corresponding to the alternative you prefer.

Follow these steps at your computer:

1. Position your cursor anywhere under the word *new*, on the last line of the paragraph.

2. Press **Alt-F1** to use the Thesaurus. Compare your screen to the one shown in Figure 8.3.

3. Observe that the Thesaurus column that contains words is divided into two sections. The upper section contains synonyms of *new;* the lower section contains antonyms of *new.* Notice that the list of antonyms concludes with the word *used* at the top of the second column.

4. Choose **1** Replace Word, and type **e** or **E** to replace *new* with *current.*

5. Save the document as MYCHAP8.LRN and clear the typing area.

CHAPTER SUMMARY

In this chapter, you learned how to use WordPerfect's Speller and Thesaurus to help you write more efficiently and accurately. You also learned how to use hyphenation to improve the appearance of justified documents.

Here's a quick technique reference for Chapter 8:

Feature or Action	How to Do It
Speller	**Ctrl-F2** (Spell)
Check spelling for entire document	**Ctrl-F2** (Spell), **3** Document
Check spelling of a single word	**Ctrl-F2** (Spell), **1** Word
Look up the spelling of a word	**Ctrl-F2** (Spell), **5** Look Up
Turn hyphenation on or off	**Shift-F8**, **1** Line (Format Line), **1** Hyphenation, **Y** or **N**
Hard hyphen	**-** (Hyphen)
Hyphen	**Home,-** (Home - hyphen)
Dash	**Home, -, -** (Home, hyphen, hyphen)
Cancel hyphenation for a single word	Position cursor on first letter of word, then press **Home- /** (Home - forward slash)
Thesaurus	Position cursor on word, press **Alt-F1**, ← or → (to move between word-choice columns), **1** Replace Word

A final reminder: Always remember to save your document before you use the Speller or Thesaurus. That way, you'll be sure to save the document before you correct it; if anything goes wrong, you can retrieve the original. You should also save the final corrected document.

CHAPTER NINE:
TABLES

If you want to arrange information in a table, you could do so by setting tabs. Setting tabs, however, is a slow and tricky process; you must figure out exactly how the table should look, measure the width of each column, and then set tabs that correspond to each measurement. You could also run into problems if your text does not fit within your tabs.

WordPerfect's Table feature allows you to create rows and columns of information without having to set tabs. You can use this feature to present data effectively, create forms such as invoices, and even do calculations in a table. When you are finished with this chapter, you will be able to:

- Create a table
- Edit and format a table
- Apply simple formulas to numbers in tables

AN OVERVIEW OF THE TABLE FEATURE

Tables consist of horizontal *rows* and vertical *columns*, as shown in Figure 9.1. In WordPerfect, the intersection of a row and a column is a *cell*. Cells are labeled with a letter followed by a number. The letter refers to the column, from left to right, and the number refers to the row, from top to bottom. For example, cell A4 in Figure 9.1 is at the intersection of the first column (A) and the fourth row (4).

Figure 9.1 **Table elements**

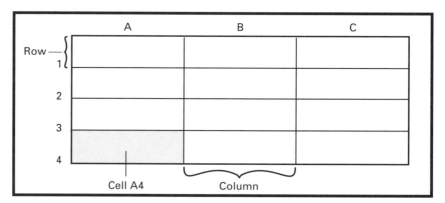

WordPerfect creates a table according to default settings. By default, the "skeleton" of rows and columns, the table's *structure*, is displayed as solid horizontal and vertical lines; these lines print with the table. The outside borders of the table are double lines, and any text you add is aligned flush left in a cell. You can change these and other defaults according to your needs. (Changing these defaults is discussed in "Editing the Table.")

WordPerfect has two modes for working with tables. In the normal editing mode, you can enter, delete, insert, and block text in a cell just as you would in the typing area. In the *Table Edit mode*, you can change the structure of the table but not enter or edit text. You can enhance text (center, underline, apply bold, and so on) in either mode.

MOVING THE CURSOR IN A TABLE IN NORMAL EDITING MODE

The cursor occupies one character position in the normal editing mode and works as it does in the normal typing area, with the following exceptions:

- Press Tab to move one cell to the right. Tabbing at the end of one row moves you to the beginning of the next.

- Press Shift-Tab to move one cell to the left. Shift-tabbing at the beginning of one row moves you to the end of the previous one.

Follow these steps at your computer:

1. Retrieve CHAP9A.LRN from your Data Disk.

2. Move to the top of page 3 by pressing **PgDn** twice.

3. Look closely at the table (Figure 9.2). It contains columns and rows, intersecting in cells. Observe the solid lines that separate rows and columns. The solid lines print with the table by default but can be changed to another pattern or removed.

4. Move to the cell labeled *POSITION*, the first cell in the table, using ↓.

5. Tab one cell to the right.

6. Examine the status line. The cursor is in cell B1, the intersection of the second column and the first row.

7. Press **Tab** several times until you reach cell B2.

8. Press **Shift-Tab** to move the cursor to the left, to cell A2.

9. Press **Shift-Tab** again to move up one row, to cell C1.

10. Press ↓ to move down one cell, to cell C2.

11. Move to the *R* in *Regional* in cell A2 by pressing **Shift-Tab** twice.

Figure 9.2   Sample table (from CHAP9A.LRN)

```
    C.   Available Positions

The following is a list of available positions and offices, and the

dates by which they must be filled:

┌─────────────────────┬────────────────────────┬──────────────────┐
│      POSITION       │        OFFICE          │   CLOSING DATE    │
├─────────────────────┼────────────────────────┼──────────────────┤
│ Regional Office     │ Atlanta Office         │ September 6       │
│ Manager             │ 367 Randwich Rd.       │                   │
│                     │ Atlanta, GA   36301    │                   │
├─────────────────────┼────────────────────────┼──────────────────┤
│ Statewide Sales     │ Chicago Office         │ July 10           │
│                     │ 1135 College Ave.      │                   │
│                     │ Chicago, IL   66604    │                   │
├─────────────────────┼────────────────────────┼──────────────────┤
│ District Production │ La Jolla Office        │ June 30           │
│ Manager             │ 46 Lindell Blvd.       │                   │
│                     │ La Jolla, CA   93108   │                   │
└─────────────────────┴────────────────────────┴──────────────────┘

Contact Marlene Marques for more information.

A:\CHAP9A.LRN                                  Doc 1 Pg 3 Ln 1" Pos 1"
```

MOVING THE CURSOR WITHIN A CELL

To move the cursor within a cell in the normal editing mode:

- Press Home, ← to move to the beginning of a line of text.
- Press Home, → to move to the end of a line of text.
- Press Ctrl-Home, ↑ to move to the beginning of text in a cell.
- Press Ctrl-Home, ↓ to move to the last line of text in a cell.

With your cursor in cell A2, follow these steps at your computer:

1. Press **Home**, → to move to the end of the line of text.
2. Press **Home**, ← to move to the beginning of the line of text.
3. Press ↓ to move to the next line of text.

ADDITIONAL CURSOR-MOVEMENT TECHNIQUES

Other techniques allow you to move quickly in one direction in a table:

- Press Ctrl-Home (Goto), Home, ↑ to move to the first cell in a column.

- Press Ctrl-Home (Goto), Home, ↓ to move to the last cell in a column.

- Press Ctrl-Home (Goto), Home, ← to move to the first cell in a row.

- Press Ctrl-Home (Goto), Home, → to move to the last cell in a row.

- Press Ctrl-Home (Goto), Home, Home, ↑ to move to the first cell in the table.

- Press Ctrl-Home (Goto), Home, Home, ↓ to move to the last cell in the table.

INSERTING AND DELETING TEXT IN A CELL

Just as WordPerfect is normally in Insert mode when you're in the typing area, it is also in Insert mode when you're in the normal editing mode. This means that if you want to insert text in your table, simply position your cursor, and type. Keystrokes you would normally use to delete text work the same way. For example, press Del to delete the character positioned at the cursor.

Follow these steps at your computer:

1. Press ↓ to position the cursor in the *Statewide Sales* cell.

2. Press **Home**, → to move to the end of the text line after the word *Sales*.

3. Press **Spacebar**, and type **Coordinator**. The text wraps to the next line of the same cell.

4. Press ↓ to move down one cell to *District Production* and position the cursor on *Production*.

5. Press **Ctrl-Backspace** to delete the word *Production*. *Manager* now appears on the first line of the cell.

CREATING A TABLE

You can create a table in the typing area, whether you're starting from a blank screen or an existing document, by following these general steps:

- Position the cursor where you want the table to begin.

- Press the Columns/Table keys, Alt-F7, to display the Table Edit menu. Choose 2 Tables and 1 Create.

- Enter the number of columns that you want the table to contain; the maximum is 32.

- Enter the number of rows that you want the table to contain; the maximum is 32,765.

When you create a table, your cursor is positioned in the Table Edit menu.

With the document CHAP9A.LRN in your typing area, follow these steps at your computer:

1. Move to the blank line above *III. PERSONNEL CHANGES* on page 2.

2. Press **Alt-F7** (Columns/Table). Notice the prompt:

   1 Columns; 2 Tables; 3 Math: Ø

3. Choose **2 T**ables to display the Table menu.

4. Choose **1 C**reate. WordPerfect suggests *3* as the default number of columns:

   Number of Columns: 3

5. Type **2** to create two columns, and press **Enter**. WordPerfect suggests *1* as the default number of rows:

   Number of Rows: 1

6. Type **3** to create three rows and press **Enter**. The table and the Table Edit menu appear. Compare your screen to the one shown in Figure 9.3.

 MOVING THE CURSOR IN TABLE EDIT MODE

In Table Edit mode, the cursor occupies (highlights) an entire cell. To move the cursor in Table Edit mode (Alt-F7):

- Press ↑, ↓, ←, or → to move one cell up, down, left, or right, respectively.

- Press Home, ↑ to move to the first cell in a column.

- Press Home, ↓ to move to the last cell in a column.

- Press Home, ← to move to the first cell in a row.

Figure 9.3   **A new table**

```
to two salespeople who have proven themselves to their peers.
The sales teams nominate and elect from themselves the recipients
of the award.  It has become the highest honor a salesperson can
receive at Macco Plastics, Inc.  This year's award recipients
follow:

  ┌──────────────────────────────┬────────────────────────────┐
  │ ████████████████████████████ │                            │
  ├──────────────────────────────┼────────────────────────────┤
  │                              │                            │
  ├──────────────────────────────┼────────────────────────────┤
  │                              │                            │
  └──────────────────────────────┴────────────────────────────┘

III. PERSONNEL CHANGES

Table Edit:   Press Exit when done        Cell A1 Doc 1 Pg 2 Ln 5.14" Pos 1.12"
─────────────────────────────────────────────────────────────────────
Ctrl-Arrows Column Widths; Ins Insert; Del Delete; Move Move/Copy;
1 Size; 2 Format; 3 Lines; 4 Header; 5 Math; 6 Options; 7 Join; 8 Split; 0
```

- Press Home, → to move to the last cell in a row.
- Press Home, Home, ↑ to move to the first cell in the table.
- Press Home, Home, ↓ to move to the last cell in the table.
- Press Ctrl-Home (Goto), and type a cell location (for example, a2 or A2) to move to a specific location. In specifying a cell, you can type either lowercase or uppercase letter (column) designations.

With the cursor positioned in the table, follow these steps at your computer:

1. Observe that an entire cell is selected. Examine the status line. The selected cell is A1.

2. Press ↓ twice to move down two cells to the last row. Confirm that this is cell A3.

3. Press → to move one cell to the right. Confirm that this is cell B3.

4. Press **Home**, ↑ to move to the first cell in the column, B1.

5. Press **Home**, ↓ to move to the last cell in the column, B3.

6. Press **Ctrl-Home** (Goto). WordPerfect prompts:

   Go to

7. Type **a1** and press **Enter**. The cursor moves to cell A1.

1. Press **Home**, **Home**, ↓ and observe where the cursor moves.

2. Press **Home**, **Home**, ↑ and observe where the cursor moves.

TYPING TEXT FOR THE TABLE

Before you enter text into the table, you need to leave the Table Edit menu by pressing the Exit key, F7. With your cursor positioned in the correct cell, begin typing.

Follow these steps at your computer:

1. Move to the first blank cell (if necessary).

2. Press **F7** to leave the Table Edit menu.

3. With **Caps Lock** on, type **RECIPIENT** and tab to the blank cell to the right, B1.

4. Type **LOCATION**, and tab to the first cell of the next row, A2.

5. With **Caps Lock** off, type **George Schwartz**, and tab to the next cell.

1. Complete the table as shown in Figure 9.4.

2. Save the document as MYCHAP9A.LRN, and remain in the typing area.

EDITING THE TABLE

When working with a table, you will often want to insert or delete columns or rows. These structural changes are made using the Table Edit menu. To display that menu in normal editing mode, position the cursor anywhere in the table and press the Columns/-Table keys, Alt-F7.

Figure 9.4   **Table with text**

```
quotas year after year.  The Harvey Mudd award is given to two

salespeople who have proven themselves to their peers.  The sales

teams nominate and elect from themselves the recipients of the

award.  It has become the highest honor a salesperson can receive

at Macco Plastics, Inc.  This year's award recipients follow:

┌─────────────────────────────┬──────────────────────────────┐
│RECIPIENT                    │LOCATION                      │
├─────────────────────────────┼──────────────────────────────┤
│George Schwartz              │Washington, D.C.              │
├─────────────────────────────┼──────────────────────────────┤
│Loretta Nelson               │Dallas                        │
└─────────────────────────────┴──────────────────────────────┘

III. PERSONNEL CHANGES


     A.   New Positions

A:\CHAP9A.LRN                         Cell B3 Doc 1 Pg 2 Ln 5.37" Pos 4.95"
```

INSERTING ROWS AND COLUMNS

To insert a row or a column:

- Display the Table Edit menu.

- Place the cursor in the row or column just past where you want to insert the new row or column.

- Press Ins.

- Choose 1 Rows or 2 Columns from the Table Edit menu.

- Type the number of rows or columns you need, and press Enter. The new row or column is inserted *before* the row or column with the cursor.

The new row or column has the same settings, such as row height or column width, as the row or column with the cursor. Although WordPerfect normally gives a new column the same width as the one with the cursor, if the table already extends to the right margin, the last column is split to make room for the new one.

With your cursor positioned inside the table, follow these steps at your computer:

1. Press **Alt-F7** to display the Table Edit menu.

2. Move to the column labeled *LOCATION*.

3. Press **Ins**. WordPerfect prompts

   `Insert: 1 Rows; 2 Columns: 0`

4. Choose **2 C**olumns. WordPerfect displays the default:

   `Number of Columns: 1`

5. Press **Enter** to accept the default and insert one column. Observe that the column was inserted to the left of the column where the cursor was positioned.

6. Press **F7** to leave the Table Edit menu.

7. In cell B3, type **President's Award.** Notice how the word *Award* wraps to the next line.

8. In cell B2, again type **President's Award.**

9. In cell B1, type **AWARD**, the column heading.

10. Move to cell A2, the cell that contains the name *George Schwartz.*

11. Press **Alt-F7** to display the Table Edit menu.

12. Press **Ins**, and choose **1 R**ows. WordPerfect displays the default:

    `Number of Rows: 1`

13. Type **3** and press **Enter** to insert three blank rows. Observe that the rows were inserted above the *George Schwartz* row.

14. Press **F7** to leave the Table Edit menu.

15. Press ↓ to drop one blank row after the title row.

16. Type **Alice Johnson**, and tab to the next cell.

17. Type **Harvey Mudd Award**, and tab to the next cell.

18. Type **Chicago**, and tab to the next row.

PRACTICE YOUR SKILLS

Enter the following text in the new row: **Leslie Wu, Harvey Mudd Award, San Francisco.**

DELETING A ROW OR COLUMN

To delete a row or a column:

- Display the Table Edit menu.

- Position the cursor in the column or row you wish to delete, and press Del.

- Choose 1 Rows or 2 Columns from the Table Edit menu.

- Counting downward for rows or to the right for columns (including the row or column containing the cursor), type the number of rows or columns you wish to delete, and press Enter. Any text within the column or row will also be deleted.

Follow these steps at your computer:

1. Move the cursor to cell A2 of the blank row.

2. Press **Alt-F7** to display the Table Edit menu.

3. Press **Del**, and choose **1 R**ows. WordPerfect displays the default:

   Number of Rows: 1

4. Press **Enter** to accept the default and delete the row.

 ADDING A COLUMN TO THE END OF A TABLE

To add or delete a row or a column at the end of a table:

- From the Table Edit menu, choose 1 Size.

- Choose either 1 Rows or 2 Columns. WordPerfect displays the number of rows or columns that are currently in the table (for example, *3*).

- Type the total number of rows or columns that you want in the table. For example, type 4 to add one column to a three-column table.

With the Table Edit menu displayed (Alt-F7), follow these steps at your computer:

1. Move to the column with the heading *LOCATION* (if necessary).

2. Choose **1 S**ize to display the Table Size menu.

3. Choose **2 C**olumns. WordPerfect displays the current setting:

   `Number of Columns: 3`

4. Type **4** and press **Enter**. The table now has four columns; one blank column was added to the right side of the table.

5. Observe the text in the third column. The column width was split in half to accommodate the fourth column, as shown in Figure 9.5.

Figure 9.5   **Column added to table**

```
┌──────────────────────────────────────────────────────────────────┐
│ ║RECIPIENT            │AWARD         │LOCATI │█████│                │
│ ║                     │              │ON     │█████│                │
│ ║─────────────────────┼──────────────┼───────┼─────┤               │
│ ║Alice Johnson        │Harvey Mudd   │Chicag │     │                │
│ ║                     │Award         │o      │     │                │
│ ║─────────────────────┼──────────────┼───────┼─────┤               │
│ ║Leslie Wu            │Harvey Mudd   │San    │     │                │
│ ║                     │Award         │Franci │     │                │
│ ║                     │              │sco    │     │                │
│ ║─────────────────────┼──────────────┼───────┼─────┤               │
│ ║George Schwartz      │President's   │Washin │     │                │
│ ║                     │Award         │gton,  │     │                │
│ ║                     │              │D.C.   │     │                │
│ ║─────────────────────┼──────────────┼───────┼─────┤               │
│ ║Loretta Nelson       │President's   │Dallas │     │                │
│ ║                     │Award         │       │     │                │
└──────────────────────────────────────────────────────────────────┘

III. PERSONNEL CHANGES

Table Edit:   Press Exit when done        Cell D1 Doc 1 Pg 2 Ln 5.14" Pos 6.78"
─────────────────────────────────────────────────────────────────────────────
Ctrl-Arrows Column Widths; Ins Insert; Del Delete; Move Move/Copy;
1 Size; 2 Format; 3 Lines; 4 Header; 5 Math; 6 Options; 7 Join; 8 Split: 0
```

PRACTICE YOUR SKILLS

Delete the column that was just inserted. The third column width stays reduced; you will widen it in the next activity.

FORMATTING CELLS AND COLUMNS

WordPerfect provides you with many ways of formatting cells and columns in a table. If, for example, a column heading is too wide for the column, you can widen the column. You can also center the heading, change its type size and style, and so on. In Table Edit mode, you can both modify the structure of a table and enhance the text it contains.

- To apply a particular format (such as centering, justifying, or underlining text), select the Format option from the Table Edit menu.

- To format a single cell, position the cursor within the cell, and select the Format option.

- To format a group of cells, first block the cells using Alt-F4, and then select the Format option.

- To format a column, position the cursor in one cell of that column, and select the Format option and 2 Column.

 COLUMN WIDTH

When you create a table, WordPerfect bases the default column widths on the current margins and the number of columns selected. Column widths can be changed in two ways, by menu and by special keystrokes. When you *increase* the width of a column, WordPerfect widens the entire table until the right margin is reached, then decreases the widest column to the right of the increased column. When you *decrease* the width of a column, the table width decreases from the right.

Changing Column Widths with the Menu
To change the column width by using the menu:

- Position the cursor within the column that you want to widen.

- Display the Table Edit menu.

- Choose 2 Format.

- Choose 2 Column.

- Choose 1 Width.

- Enter the desired measurement.

With the Table Edit menu displayed, follow these steps at your computer:

1. Move to the column labeled *RECIPIENT.*

2. Choose **2** Format to display the Format menu.

3. Choose **2** Column to display the Columns menu.

4. Choose **1 W**idth. WordPerfect displays the current setting:

```
Column width: 3.25"
```

5. Type **2.25**, and press **Enter**. The column width is decreased by an inch. The size of the table decreases accordingly.

Changing Column Widths with Keys

You can change the column width a character at a time by using key combinations. This is useful if you want to refine your table structure but don't know what fraction of an inch to use.

- Press Ctrl-→ to increase the column width by one character.

- Press Ctrl-← to decrease the column width by one character.

With the Table Edit menu displayed, follow these steps at your computer:

1. Move to any cell in the column labeled *AWARD*.

2. Press **Ctrl-→**. The column increases by one character.

3. Continue pressing **Ctrl-→** until all text fits on one line within each cell.

PRACTICE YOUR SKILLS

1. Move to the cell labeled *LOCATION*.

2. Increase the cell width until all text fits on one line.

 COLUMN AND CELL FORMATTING

In normal editing mode, you can enhance text in columns and cells in your table just as you would regular text. You can also do this in Table Edit mode, through the Table Edit menu. To format table text in Table Edit mode, you must use the formats found in the Table Edit menu; you cannot, for example, use Shift-F6 to center text while you're in a table.

Centering a Column Heading

To center a column heading:

- Position your cursor in the cell containing the heading.

- Choose 2 Format.

- Choose 1 Cell.

- Choose 3 Justify.

- Choose 2 Center.

With the Table Edit menu displayed, follow these steps at your computer:

1. Move to cell A1 by pressing **Ctrl-Home**, typing **a1**, and pressing **Enter**.

2. Choose **2** **F**ormat to display the Format menu.

3. Choose **1** **C**ell to display the Cell menu.

4. Choose **3** **J**ustify to display the Justification menu.

5. Choose **2** **C**enter. The heading *RECIPIENT* is centered.

Centering Cell Text

To center text in a cell, press Alt-F7 to enter Table Edit mode, and follow these steps:

- Position your cursor in the cell containing the text you want to center.

- Use the Block feature (Alt-F4) to highlight the text.

- Choose 2 Format.

- Choose 1 Cell.

- Choose 3 Justify.

- Choose 2 Center.

With the Table Edit menu displayed, follow these steps at your computer:

1. Press → to move to cell B1.

2. Highlight the next cell by pressing **Alt-F4** and →.

3. Choose **2** **F**ormat to display the Format menu.

4. Choose **1** **C**ell to display the Cell menu.

5. Choose **3** **J**ustify to display the Justification menu.

6. Choose **2** **C**enter to center the blocked headings.

Justifying Text Within a Column

To format text in a column, position the cursor in *any* cell in that column before selecting a formatting command. To justify text within a column, press Alt-F7 and follow these steps:

- Position the cursor in any cell of the column you wish to justify.

- Choose 2 Format.

- Choose 2 Column.

- Choose 3 Justify.

- Choose 1 Left (WordPerfect's default setting), 2 Center, 3 Right, or 4 Full.

With the Table Edit menu displayed, follow these steps at your computer:

1. Move your cursor anywhere within the column labeled *LOCATION*.

2. Choose **2** Format to display the Format menu.

3. Choose **2** Column to display the Column menu.

4. Choose **3** Justify to display the Justification menu.

5. Choose **3** Right. The text in the entire column is right-aligned, except for the heading *LOCATION*, which retains its earlier, centered formatting.

To override any previous formatting for a cell, position the cursor within the cell, choose 2 Format, 1 Cell (instead of 2 column), and so on. Notice that formatting a single *cell* overrides any previous *column* formatting that was applied to that cell.

Enhancing Cell Text

You can apply formatting such as underline and bold to text in a cell by following these general steps:

- Position your cursor in the cell with the text you wish to format.

- Choose 2 Format.

- Choose 1 Cell.

- Choose 2 Attributes.

- Choose 2 Appearance.

- Choose an Appearance option, such as 1 Bold or 7 Sm Cap.

With the Table Edit menu displayed, follow these steps at your computer:

1. Move your cursor to the column heading *RECIPIENT.*

2. Choose **2 F**ormat to display the Format menu.

3. Choose **1 C**ell to display the Column menu.

4. Choose **2 A**ttributes to display the Attributes menu.

5. Choose **2 A**ppearance.

6. Choose **2 U**ndln. The heading is underlined.

PRACTICE YOUR SKILLS

Underline the remaining column headings.

LINES

The Lines option in the Table Edit menu enables you to change the appearance of cell borders in a table. The Block key, Alt-F4, is used to block the cells whose borders you wish to change in the same way; otherwise, only the cell containing the cursor is affected.

The Lines menu displays the following choices to control which cell borders are changed.

Left	**Left Border of the Cell or Blocked Cells**
Right	Right border of the cell or blocked cells
Top	Top border of the cell or blocked cells
Bottom	Bottom border of the cell or blocked cells
Inside	Inside borders of the cell or blocked cells
Outside	Outside borders of the cell or blocked cells
All	Inside and outside borders of the cell or blocked cells

Inside lines separate cells from one another. *Outside* lines separate the block from the rest of the table. To see what the borders look like before you print, leave the Table Edit menu, and choose 6 - View Document from the Print menu (Shift-F7).

Removing the Table Lines

To remove the inside lines from a group of cells in a table:

- Position your cursor at one corner of the range of cells you wish to define.

- Highlight the range of cells whose lines you wish to remove.

- Choose 3 Lines.

- Choose 5 Inside.

- Choose 1 None.

With the Table Edit menu displayed, follow these steps at your computer:

1. Move your cursor to cell A1.

2. Highlight the text from cell A1 through cell C5. (Press **Alt-F4** to block, then press → twice and ↓ four times.)

3. Choose **3 L**ines to display the Lines menu.

4. Choose **5 I**nside.

5. Choose **1 N**one. All the lines on the inside of the table are removed.

 CENTERING THE TABLE BETWEEN THE LEFT AND RIGHT MARGINS

Selecting Options in the Table Edit menu enables you to position a table in relation to the right and left margins. The default setting, *Full*, causes the table to fill the space between the left and right margins. *Left* aligns the table with the left margin; *Right* aligns the table with the right margin; and *Center* centers the table between the left and right margins.

To center the table on the page:

- Choose 6 Options.

- Choose 3 - Position of Table.

- Choose 3 Center.

- Press F7 twice—once to return to the Table Edit menu, and once again to return to the typing area.

With the Table Edit menu displayed, follow these steps at your computer:

1. Press **F7** to return to the **Table Edit** menu.

2. View the document by pressing **Shift-F7** and choosing **6 - V**iew Document. The table is now flush with the left margin.

3. Press **F7** to return to the typing area.

4. Press **Alt-F7** to display the Table Edit menu.

5. Choose **6 O**ptions to display the Table Options menu.

6. Choose **3 - P**osition of Table to display the Table Position menu.

7. Choose **3 C**enter to center the table between the margins.

8. Press **F7** to return to the Table Edit menu, and press **F7** once more to leave the Table Edit menu. The table is now centered between the left and right margins.

9. Exit to the typing area.

10. Save the document under the same name, and clear the typing area.

MATH IN TABLES

Until now, you've been entering only text into your table. WordPerfect is especially powerful if you work with numbers. The Math feature enables you to enter numbers, apply formulas to your data, and do simple calculations, such as subtotals. All math operations are done through the Table Edit menu (Alt-F7).

 ENTERING NUMBERS IN A TABLE

To enter numbers into your table, position the cursor on the cell in which you wish to enter a number, and type. Follow these steps at your computer:

1. Retrieve CHAP9B.LRN.

2. Scroll to the bottom of page 1, using ↓ to display a second table. Notice that the table is not formatted.

3. Move to cell B5 in the *ADVANCES* column for Los Angeles.

4. Type **400.00**, and tab to cell C5.

5. Type **700.00**, and tab three times to cell B6.

Compare your screen to the one shown in Figure 9.6.

Figure 9.6   **Table with numbers**

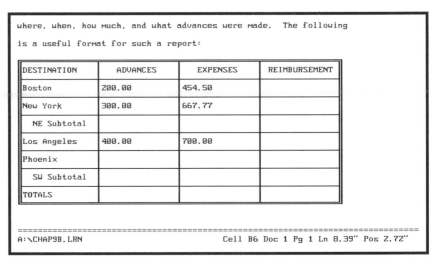

```
where, when, how much, and what advances were made.   The following
is a useful format for such a report:
```

DESTINATION	ADVANCES	EXPENSES	REIMBURSEMENT
Boston	200.00	454.50	
New York	300.00	667.77	
NE Subtotal			
Los Angeles	400.00	700.00	
Phoenix			
SW Subtotal			
TOTALS			

```
=============================================================================
A:\CHAP9B.LRN                          Cell B6 Doc 1 Pg 1 Ln 8.39" Pos 2.72"
```

SETTING A COLUMN WITH DECIMAL ALIGNMENT AND INSERTING NUMBERS

The numbers you've entered appear to be aligned at the decimal point, but only because they contain the same number of digits. If you were to enter the amount 4,000.00 in one of the cells, the decimal point would not be aligned with the decimal points of the other numbers.

To format numbers so that their decimal points are aligned, follow these steps at your computer:

1. Move your cursor to the column labeled *ADVANCES* if it's not already there.

2. Press **Alt-F7** to display the Table Edit menu.

3. Choose **2 F**ormat, and choose **2 C**olumn to display the Column menu.

4. Choose **3 J**ustify.

5. Choose **5 D**ecimal Align. The numbers for the entire column are aligned at their decimal points.

6. Move the cursor to the column labeled *EXPENSES*.

7. Repeat Steps 3-5 to align the decimals in the *EXPENSES* column. (The *REIMBURSEMENT* column, though empty, is already set for decimal alignment.)

8. Tab to cell B6.

9. Press **F7** to leave the Table Edit menu. You must leave the menu and return to normal editing mode before you can type text or numbers into a table.

10. Observe the status line. The message

    `align char = .`

    tells you that when you enter a number with a decimal point, it will align with the decimal point of the other numbers in the same column.

11. Type **350.00**. The number automatically aligns at the decimal point as you enter it into the table.

12. Press **Tab** and type **396.60**. This number, too, is aligned at its decimal point.

CALCULATING SUBTOTALS

Suppose that you need to add the *Boston* and *New York* figures to obtain subtotals for the northeast region. In WordPerfect, the operator + (plus sign) calculates subtotals, summing the values of all cells in the current column above the cursor. (You'll be learning more about WordPerfect's operators a little later on.)

Follow these steps at your computer:

1. Move your cursor to cell B4, the first *NE Subtotal* cell.

2. Press **Alt-F7** to display the Table Edit menu.

3. Choose **5 M**ath, and type **4** or **+** to choose the subtotal operator. The subtotal, 500.00, for Boston and New York is calculated.

4. Examine =+ in the bottom-left corner of the table. The left edge of the status line displays the calculation or formula, if one exists for a cell.

PRACTICE YOUR SKILLS

Find the subtotals for the rest of the table.

 FORMULAS

A formula performs an operation (such as addition) on numbers in cells you specify, and places the results of the operation in the cell where you put the formula. For example, placing the formula *A1+B1* in cell C1 adds any number in cell A1 to any number in cell B1 and displays the result in cell C1.

Entering a Formula
To enter a formula in a table:

• Position your cursor in the cell where you wish to enter the formula.

• Choose 5 Math.

• Choose 2 Formula.

• Type the formula. For example, entering *a1+a2* (or *A1+A2*) in cell A3 calculates the sum of any numbers in cells A1 and A2 and displays the results in A3.

• Press Enter.

With the Table Edit menu displayed, follow these steps at your computer:

1. Move your cursor to cell D2, the first blank cell in the *REIM-BURSEMENT* column.

2. Choose **5 M**ath to display the Math menu.

3. Choose **2** Formula. WordPerfect prompts:

   Enter formula:

4. Type **c2-b2** and press **Enter**. The result of the calculation appears in cell D2. The cell formula appears in the status line:

   =C2-B2

Copying a Formula

To repeat a formula already used in one cell in another cell, you could retype the formula. But to save time and avoid the possibility of typing errors, you can copy a formula from one cell to another. This can be useful if a subtotal, for example, must be calculated for many columns.

To copy a formula:

- Position the cursor in the cell with the formula you wish to copy.

- Choose 5 Math from the Table Edit menu.

- Choose 3 Copy Formula.

- Specify whether to copy Down or to the Right, and specify the number of times the formula should be copied. For example, if you choose *Down* and enter *3*, the formula is copied down to the next three cells.

With your cursor positioned in cell D2 and the Table Edit menu displayed, follow these steps at your computer:

1. Choose **5 M**ath to display the Math menu.

2. Choose **3** Copy Formula. You can see the prompt:

   Copy Formula To: 1 Cell; 2 Down; 3 Right: 0

3. Choose **2 D**own. Notice the prompt:

   Number of times to copy formula: 1

4. Type **5**, and press **Enter**. The formula is copied down the column (down five rows), and the reimbursements are calculated. Cell references within the formula are relative; they automatically adjust to the row into which they are copied.

 CALCULATING TOTALS IN A TABLE

The Math feature provides the following mathematical operators:

- +   finds subtotals
- =   finds totals
- *   finds grand totals

To use one of these operators in a table, you must choose it from the Math menu; you cannot type it from the keyboard.

With the Table Edit menu displayed, follow these steps at your computer:

1. Move your cursor to cell B8.

2. Choose **5 M**ath.

3. Choose **2 F**ormula. WordPerfect prompts:

   Enter formula:

4. Type **b4+b7** and press **Enter**. The total, 1250.00, is displayed in cell B8.

5. Find the totals of the remaining two cells. (Copy the formula.) Compare your screen to the one shown in Figure 9.7. At this point, you may wish to print your document. Figure 9.8 shows how the printout should look.

6. Leave the document, and save it as MYCHAP9B.LRN.

Figure 9.7   **Table with calculated totals**

```
detail where, when, how much, and what advances were made.   The
following is a useful format for such a report:

DESTINATION      ADVANCES       EXPENSES       REIMBURSEMENT
Boston             200.00        454.50            254.50
New York           300.00        667.77            367.77
  NE Subtotal      500.00      1,122.27            622.27
Los Angeles        400.00        700.00            300.00
Phoenix            350.00        396.60             46.60
  SW Subtotal      750.00      1,096.60            346.60
TOTALS           1,250.00      2,218.87            968.87

=D4+D7 Align char = .                 Cell D8 Doc 1 Pg 1 Ln 8.95" Pos 6.78"

Ctrl-Arrows Column Widths;  Ins Insert;  Del Delete;  Move Move/Copy;
1 Size; 2 Format; 3 Lines; 4 Header; 5 Math; 6 Options; 7 Join; 8 Split; 0
```

Figure 9.8   **The completed document MYCHAP9B.LRN**

C.   Available Positions

The following is a list of available positions and offices, and the dates by which they must be filled:

POSITION	OFFICE	CLOSING DATE
Regional Office Manager	Atlanta Office 367 Randwich Rd. Atlanta, GA 36301	September 6
Statewide Sales Coordinator	Chicago Office 1135 College Ave. Chicago, IL 66604	July 10
District Manager	La Jolla Office 46 Lindell Blvd. La Jolla, CA 93108	June 30

Contact Marlene Marques for more information.

IV. NEW EXPENSE REPORT FORMATS

A short note on procedures. Due to the large increase in travel by Macco employees, we are requesting that you and your staff submit a travel expense report on a quarterly basis. It should detail where, when, how much, and what advances were made. The following is a useful format for such a report:

DESTINATION	ADVANCES	EXPENSES	REIMBURSEMENT
Boston	200.00	454.50	254.50
New York	300.00	667.77	367.77
NE Subtotal	500.00	1,122.27	622.27
Los Angeles	400.00	700.00	300.00
Phoenix	350.00	396.60	46.60
SW Subtotal	750.00	1,096.60	346.60
TOTALS	1,250.00	2,218.87	968.87

V.   CONCLUSION

Overall, as you can see, it has been an impressive quarter of growth and change here at Macco. You should be proud of what you've done. Let's keep up the good work!

PRACTICE YOUR SKILLS

In this chapter, you have learned how to create and edit tables. The following activity gives you the opportunity to practice these techniques while producing the document shown in Figure 9.9 from the original document, PRAC9.LRN.

Figure 9.9   **The completed document MYPRAC9.LRN**

MOOSIE'S GARDEN PATCH

Organic and Pure

Product Line Announcement

<u>Introduction</u>

Moosie's Garden Patch is pleased to announce the unveiling of a new fruit line in the Garden Patch series: the Fruit Patch. The Fruit Patch product line was developed through the cooperation and dedication of Dr.'s Eugene Alfa and Vera Betta and their staffs after two years of intense work. The FDA recently approved the food and it will be released for public sale in three weeks.

The Fruit Patch includes a variety of organically grown fruit: the berries (cherries, strawberries, raspberries, blackberries, and blueberries), apricots, peaches, grapes, and plums.

<u>Projected Quarterly Sales</u>

Our finance department has been hard at work, determining sales projections for the next quarter. Those results are shown below in the table.

Projected Quarterly Sales Table

Vendors and Brokers	Boxes Sold	Profit-Each
Trader Tom's	2,300	1.49
Aunt Emily's Market	4,900	1.29
Hamlet Farms	6,500	1.09
B & J's	10,000	.79
Hout, Black, & Wallace Inc	11,500	.79
Totals	35,200.00	

Follow these steps at your computer:

1. Clear the typing area, and retrieve the file PRAC9.LRN.

2. Move your cursor to the table at the bottom of page 1, and type the following information (in bold) into the table:

	Column 1	Column 2	Column 3
Row 3	**Trader Tom's**	**2,300**	**1.49**
Row 4	**Aunt Emily's Market**	**4,900**	**1.29**
Row 5	**Hamlet Farms**	**6,500**	**1.09**

3. Delete the row that contains information for Price Farms Co.

4. Center the column headings *Vendors and Brokers*, *Boxes Sold*, and *Profit-Each*.

5. Change the column width for the *Boxes Sold* column to 1.43". Change the column width for *Profit-Each* to 1.63".

6. Decimal-align the *Boxes Sold* and *Profit-Each* columns.

7. Move to the row containing *Totals* and find the subtotal for *Boxes Sold*.

8. Save the document as MYPRAC9.LRN.

9. Print the document, and compare it to the one shown in Figure 9.9.

If you have finished the above activity and would like to try another one that requires similar skills but provides less guidance, follow the steps below, editing the file OPT9.LRN to match the document shown in Figure 9.10.

1. Retrieve the file OPT9.LRN.

2. Add a column to the end of the table.

3. Increase the width of the last column (the column you added in Step 2) to 1.61".

4. Increase the width of third column until *Profit-Each* fits on one line.

5. Move to the first cell in the last column, and type the heading **Total Profit**. Remember to leave Table Edit mode before typing.

Figure 9.10   **The completed document MYOPT9.LRN**

MOOSIE'S GARDEN PATCH

Organic and Pure

Product Line Announcement

<u>Introduction</u>

Moosie's Garden Patch is pleased to announce the unveiling of a
new fruit line in the Garden Patch series: the Fruit Patch. The
Fruit Patch product line was developed through the cooperation
and dedication of Dr.'s Eugenie Alfa and Vera Betta and their
staffs after two years of intense work. The FDA recently approved
the food and it will be released for public sale in three weeks.

The Fruit Patch includes a variety of organically grown fruit:
the berries (cherries, strawberries, raspberries, blackberries,
and blueberries), apricots, peaches, grapes, and plums.

<u>Projected Quarterly Sales</u>

Our finance department has been hard at work, determining sales
projections for the next quarter. Those results are shown below
in the table.

Projected Quarterly Sales Table

Vendors and Brokers	Boxes Sold	Profit-Each	Total Profit
Trader Tom's	2,300	1.49	3,427.00
Aunt Emily's Market	4,900	1.29	6,321.00
Hamlet Farms	6,500	1.09	7,085.00
B & J's	10,000	.79	7,900.00
Hout, Black, & Wallace Inc	11,500	.79	9,085.00
Totals	35,200.00		33,818.00

6. Find the total profit for *Trader Tom's* by entering a formula. Use the operator * in your formula to calculate the grand total.

7. Copy the formula down the column to find the total profit for the remaining vendors.

8. Find the subtotal of the *Total Profit* column.

9. Center the table on the page.

10. Save the document as MYOPT9.LRN

11. Print the document, and compare it to the one shown in Figure 9.10.

CHAPTER SUMMARY

In this chapter, you've learned much useful information about creating and editing a table. You've explored how to edit and enhance text in a table and to refine a table's structure. You've also learned to enter numbers and perform math calculations in a table.

Here's a quick technique reference for Chapter 9:

Feature or Action	How to Do It
Normal Editing Mode	
Move one cell to the right	**Tab**
Move one cell to the left	**Shift-Tab**
Move to the beginning of a line	**Home, ←**
Move to the end of a line	**Home, →**
Move to the beginning of text in a cell	**Ctrl-Home, ↑**
Move to the last line of text in a cell	**Ctrl-Home, ↓**
Move to the first cell in a column	**Ctrl-Home, Home, ↑**
Move to the last cell in a column	**Ctrl-Home, Home, ↓**
Move to the first cell in a row	**Ctrl-Home, Home, ←**
Move to the last cell in a row	**Ctrl-Home, Home, →**

Feature or Action	How to Do It
Move to the first cell in the table	**Ctrl-Home, Home, Home, ↑**
Move to the last cell in the table	**Ctrl-Home, Home, Home, ↓**

Table Edit Mode

Feature or Action	How to Do It
Move one cell up, down, left, or right	**↑, ↓, ←, or →**
Move to the first cell in a column	**Home, ↑**
Move to the last cell in a column	**Home, ↓**
Move to the first cell in a row	**Home, ←**
Move to the last cell in a row	**Home, →**
Move to the first cell in the table	**Home, Home, ↑**
Move to the last cell in the table	**Home, Home, ↓**
Move to a specific cell	**Ctrl-Home** (Goto), <cell identifier (for example, A2)>
Create a table	**Alt-F7** (Columns/Table), **2 T**ables, **1 C**reate, <number of columns>, **Enter**, <number of rows>, **Enter**
Insert rows and columns	**Alt-F7** (Columns/Table), **Ins**, **1 R**ows or **2 C**olumns, <number of rows or columns to be inserted>, **Enter**
Delete rows and columns	**Alt-F7** (Columns/Table), **Del**, **1 R**ows or **2 C**olumns, <number of rows or columns to be deleted>, **Enter**

Feature or Action	How to Do It
Insert or delete rows and columns at the end of a table	**Alt-F7** (Columns/Table), **1 S**ize, **1 R**ows or **2 C**olumns, <total number of rows or columns that you want in the table>, **Enter**
Change column width	**Alt-F7** (Columns/Table), **2 F**ormat, **2 C**olumn, **1 W**idth, <measurement in inches>; **Ctrl-→** (increase a character at a time); **Ctrl-←** (decrease a character at a time)
Center text in a cell	**Alt-F7** (Columns/Table), **2 F**ormat, **1 C**ell, **3 J**ustify, **2 C**enter
Right-align text in a cell	**Alt-F7** (Columns/Table), **2 F**ormat, **1 C**ell, **3 J**ustify, **3 R**ight
Underline cell text	**Alt-F7** (Columns/Table), **2 F**ormat, **1 C**ell, **2 A**ttributes, **2 A**ppearance, **2 U**ndln
Remove inside table lines	**Alt-F7** (Columns/Table), **Alt-F4** (Block), highlight the range of cells, **3 L**ines, **5 I**nside, **1 N**one
Center the table between the left and right margins	**Alt-F7** (Columns/Table), **6 O**ptions, **3 - P**osition of Table, **3 C**enter, **F7**
Enter a math formula	**Alt-F7** (Columns/Table), **5 M**ath, **2 F**ormula, <formula>, **Enter**
Copy a formula	**Alt-F7** (Columns/Table), **5 M**ath, **3 C**opy a Formula, **D**own or **R**ight, <number of cells>
Decimal-align numbers	**Alt-F7** (Columns/Table), **2 F**ormat, **2 C**olumn, **3 J**ustify, **5 D**ecimal Align
Use a mathematical operator	**Alt-F7** (Columns/Table), **5 M**ath, <number corresponding to operator>

In the next chapter, you'll learn how to use WordPerfect's Merge feature to make your form letters more personal.

CHAPTER TEN: MERGING DOCUMENTS

Creating a Primary
File and Entering
Merge Codes

Creating a
Secondary File

Merging Primary
and Secondary
Files

Merging from the
Keyboard

In word processing, *merging* or *mail-merge* is the process of transferring selected information from one document to another document. For example, you can write a form letter and instantly merge it with your mailing list to produce a customized letter for everyone on the mailing list. Other common mail-merge documents include mailing labels and interoffice memos. In Chapter 11 you will learn how to make mailing labels.

Before using WordPerfect's Merge feature, you should be familiar with two important terms. The *primary file* is the document containing all the information that remains the same. In the case of a form letter, the primary file contains the content of the letter, without the names and addresses that vary from letter to letter. The *secondary file* contains the variable information that is placed selectively in the primary file. In a form letter, the secondary file is the mailing list.

To instruct WordPerfect how to merge files, you must place *Merge codes* in the primary and secondary files. In the primary file, Merge codes mark the places where the variable information from the secondary file is to be inserted; think of the Merge code as the *X* in *Dear X*. In the secondary file, Merge codes show WordPerfect how your information is organized so that it can pull in the exact kind and amount of information (Dear *Mr. Rodriguez,* for example).

In this chapter, you'll learn how to merge documents to create the form letter shown in Figure 10.1. When you are finished with this chapter, you will be able to:

- Create a primary file
- Create a secondary file
- Merge primary and secondary files
- Merge from the keyboard

Figure 10.1   **Completed Merge document**

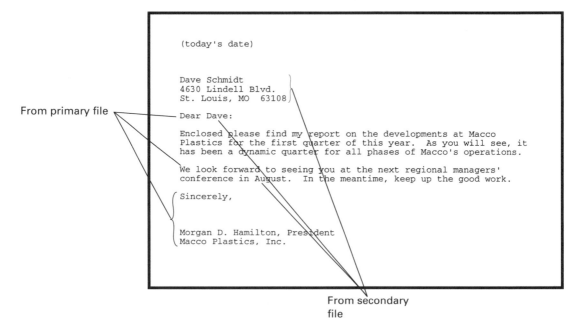

From primary file

(today's date)

Dave Schmidt
4630 Lindell Blvd.
St. Louis, MO 63108

Dear Dave:

Enclosed please find my report on the developments at Macco
Plastics for the first quarter of this year. As you will see, it
has been a dynamic quarter for all phases of Macco's operations.

We look forward to seeing you at the next regional managers'
conference in August. In the meantime, keep up the good work.

Sincerely,

Morgan D. Hamilton, President
Macco Plastics, Inc.

From secondary
file

CREATING A PRIMARY FILE AND ENTERING MERGE CODES

To merge files, begin by creating a primary file containing the standard, non-varying text you want to include in each letter. Include special *Merge codes* to identify where variable *text*—such as name and address, which vary from letter to letter—will be inserted from the secondary file. When the primary and secondary files are merged, one letter is produced for each set of data in the secondary file.

The Merge code {FIELD} marks the place in the primary file where variable information from the secondary file is inserted. *Fields* are numbered data items from the list of names and addresses in the secondary file. For example, Field 1 may contain the first name, Field 2 the last name, and so on, as shown in Figure 10.2. To insert the same first name more than once in the primary file, simply repeat the Field 1 code.

In this section you will create a primary file containing several {FIELD} codes. In the next section, you will create the secondary file—a mailing list—organized according to the field numbers you placed in the primary file. For example, in the primary file you will put {FIELD}2 where you expect to insert the recipient's last name. Later, in the secondary file, you'll need to enter the last name as the second item in each address.

In your own work, you will often create a primary file from an existing secondary file, such as a mailing list. In such cases, you must base {FIELD} codes in the primary file on the field organization of the secondary file. For example, you'll look at the secondary file to see where the last name appears in each address; if it is the second field, insert the {FIELD}2 code in the primary file wherever you want the recipient's last name to appear.

What if some addresses on your mailing list do not have an office designation? You don't want WordPerfect to leave a blank line in your letter when this occurs. To avoid spaces or blank lines in the merged document, type a question mark (*?*) after the field number in any field that might be empty for some letters, such as title or company name. Notice in Figure 10.2 that a line is left in the primary file for an office designation, {FIELD}3, and that this field is defined using a question mark. When the primary and secondary files are merged, WordPerfect ignores fields without corresponding information in the secondary file. Merging blank fields that have not used the question mark after the field number produces spaces or blank lines in the final merged document. You will learn how to use the question mark in the upcoming exercise.

Figure 10.2   **Structure of the primary file**

First Name Last Name
Office Designation
Street Address
City, State Zip Code

Dear **First Name**:

Enclosed please find my report on developments at Macco Plastics for the first quarter of this year. As you will see, it has been a dynamic quarter for all phases of Macco's operations.

We look forward to seeing you at the next regional managers' conference in **Month**. In the meantime, keep up the good work.

Sincerely,

Morgan D. Hamilton, President
Macco Plastics Inc.

{Field}1	=	First Name
{Field}2	=	Last Name
{Field}3?	=	Office Designation
{Field}4	=	Street Address
{Field}5	=	City
{Field}6	=	State
{Field}7	=	Zip Code
{Field}8	=	Month

This exercise shows you how to add Merge codes to a primary file. Follow the steps at your computer:

1. Retrieve the document PRIMLT.LRN from your Data Disk. Position the cursor at the top of the document if it is not already there.

2. Press the Merge Codes keys, **Shift-F9**.

3. Choose **1 Field**. WordPerfect prompts you to assign a number to the first field in your primary file:

   Enter Field:

4. Type **1** and press **Enter**. The Merge code {FIELD}1~ is inserted in the document.

5. Press **Spacebar** to insert a space.

6. Press **Shift-F9** to insert another field.

7. Choose **1 Field**. Again, WordPerfect prompts

   Enter Field:

8. Type **2** and press **Enter**. {FIELD}2~ (which will contain the recipient's last name) is inserted in the document.

9. Press **Enter** to begin a new line.

10. Press **Shift-F9** to insert the third field.

11. Choose **1 Field**. WordPerfect prompts

   Enter Field:

12. Type **3?** and press **Enter**. This represents the information for Field 3 (office designation), which may be blank. The *?* instructs WordPerfect to determine whether the field is blank in the secondary file. If it is blank, this line is skipped in the primary file.

13. Press **Enter** to begin a new line.

PRACTICE YOUR SKILLS

1. Insert the remaining field codes, as shown in Figure 10.3, to complete the primary file. Don't forget the {FIELD}8~ code in the second paragraph.

2. Exit the document, renaming it MYPRIMLT.LRN, and remain in WordPerfect.

Figure 10.3   **Primary file with inserted Merge codes**

```
{FIELD}1~ {FIELD}2~
{FIELD}3?~
{FIELD}4~
{FIELD}5~, {FIELD}6~  {FIELD}7~

Dear {FIELD}1~:

Enclosed please find my report on the developments at Macco
Plastics for the first quarter of this year.  As you will see, it
has been a dynamic quarter for all phases of Macco's operations.

We look forward to seeing you at the next regional managers'
conference in {FIELD}8~.  In the meantime, keep up the good work.

Sincerely,


Morgan D. Hamilton, President
Macco Plastics Inc.
```

CREATING A SECONDARY FILE

The secondary file contains *records*, each of which consists of fields. A record describes in detail a person or thing, for example, a person on a mailing list. Each field of a record contains information about a different facet of the person or thing. The number of records and sizes of fields is limited only by disk space, and each record can contain as much information—as many fields—as you need. Records are separated by an {END RECORD} code and a Hard Page code, [HPg].

To avoid confusion, all records in the secondary file must have the same field structure. For example, if Field 3 of the first record contains title information, then Field 3 of every record must either contain title information or be empty. If a record does not contain information for a certain field—you might be missing a zip code, for example—you should define it in the secondary document as an empty field by inserting an {END FIELD} code.

To create a secondary file, follow these steps at your computer:

1. From a clear screen, type **Mark** and press **F9** to insert the End Field code. The {END FIELD} code automatically advances the cursor to the next line. This field corresponds to {FIELD}1~ in the primary file.

2. Type **Short** and press **F9**. This field corresponds to {FIELD}2~ in the primary file.

3. Press **F9**. This *empty* field corresponds to {FIELD}3?~ in the primary file, and is ignored during the Merge because of the *?* in the primary file.

4. Type **367 Randwich Road** and press **F9**. This field corresponds to {FIELD}4~ in the primary file.

5. Type **Savannah** and press **F9**. This field corresponds to {FIELD}5~ in the primary file.

6. Type **GA** and press **F9**. This field corresponds to {FIELD}6~ in the primary file.

7. Type **36301** and press **F9**. This field corresponds to {FIELD}7~ in the primary file.

8. Type **July** and press **F9**. This field corresponds to {FIELD}8~ in the primary file.

9. Press **Shift-F9** (Merge Codes), and choose **2 E**nd Record to end the record and insert a Hard Page code.

Each record is considered a separate page by the program; the line of equal signs represents the hard page break. There is only one record currently displayed, so only one page break is shown.

Here are some points to remember:

- Do not separate fields or records with an extra hard return.

- Do not insert spaces between the last word in a field and an {END RECORD} or {END FIELD} code.

- Maintain the same field structure for each record. For example, in the secondary file you are now creating, Field 6 must always be a state, Field 8 must always be a month, and so on.

- Do not add any extra spaces before the {END FIELD} and {END RECORD} codes. These extra spaces will show up as extra spaces in the merged letter.

PRACTICE YOUR SKILLS

1. Complete record 2, for *Marlene Albert*, as shown in Figure 10.4.

Figure 10.4   **Secondary file with two records**

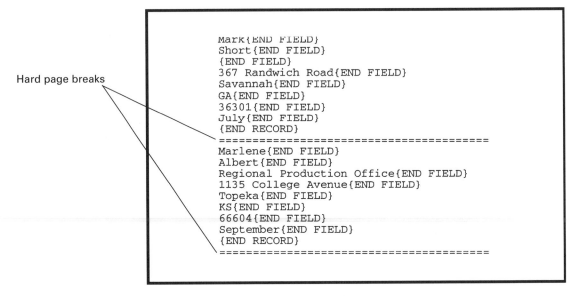

Hard page breaks

```
Mark{END FIELD}
Short{END FIELD}
{END FIELD}
367 Randwich Road{END FIELD}
Savannah{END FIELD}
GA{END FIELD}
36301{END FIELD}
July{END FIELD}
{END RECORD}
========================================
Marlene{END FIELD}
Albert{END FIELD}
Regional Production Office{END FIELD}
1135 College Avenue{END FIELD}
Topeka{END FIELD}
KS{END FIELD}
66604{END FIELD}
September{END FIELD}
{END RECORD}
========================================
```

2. Save the document as MYLIST.LRN and leave the document, but do not exit WordPerfect.

MERGING PRIMARY AND SECONDARY FILES

After you create the primary and secondary files, you can merge them to create a customized letter for each record in the secondary file. The results of the merge are displayed on the screen, and you can edit and print them like any other document. The final step is for you to merge the files and create the two personalized letters.

Follow these steps at your computer:

1. Press **Ctrl-F9** (Merge/Sort) to merge the files.

2. Choose **1 M**erge. WordPerfect prompts you to enter the name of your primary file:

   Primary file:

3. Type **myprimlt.lrn** and press **Enter**. Now WordPerfect prompts you to enter your secondary file:

   Secondary file:

4. Type **mylist.lrn** and press **Enter**. WordPerfect tells you what it is doing:

```
* Merging *
```

When WordPerfect has merged your files, the cursor is positioned at the end of the second letter.

5. Press **PgUp** to go to the top of the first letter.

6. Choose Full Document from the Print menu (Shift-F7) to print both letters created by the merge.

7. Compare the first printed letter to Figure 10.5.

Figure 10.5   **First merged document**

```
Mark Short
367 Randwich Road
Savannah, GA 36301

Dear Mark:

Enclosed  please  find  my  report  on  the developments at Macco
Plastics for the first quarter of this year.  As you will see, it
has been a dynamic quarter for all phases of Macco's operations.

We  look  forward  to  seeing  you at the next regional managers'
conference in July.  In the meantime, keep up the good work.

Sincerely,


Morgan D. Hamilton, President
Macco Plastics Inc.
```

8. Exit the document and clear the typing area without saving the file. There is no need to save the file, because the merge can easily be re-created.

MERGING FROM THE KEYBOARD

Although you always need a primary file for a merge, you do not always need a secondary file; instead, you can merge directly from the keyboard. In other words, you can type the variable information during the merge. This kind of merge is helpful when you need to create only one form letter from a primary document or when you want to include variable information not found in a secondary file. To allow information to be typed from the keyboard rather than retrieved from a file, insert the {KEYBOARD} code in the primary file. Here's how to do it:

- Press Shift-F9 (Merge Codes).

- Choose 6 More. A box appears in the upper-right corner of the screen, displaying a list of commands. Use the arrow keys or PgUp/PgDn to scroll. Commands are displayed alphabetically and can also be selected quickly by pressing the first letter of the desired command and pressing Enter.

- Highlight the {KEYBOARD} command.

- Press Enter to insert the command into the document.

Insert the {PROMPT} code in your primary file to display a message or prompt on the status line during the merge. This message, which you write, serves as a reminder or provides direction to you or the person doing the merge. The {PROMPT} code must be followed by a {KEYBOARD} code if you would like the merge to stop temporarily to allow for typing. For example, you could insert the line

```
{PROMPT} Type the memo now~{KEYBOARD}
```

in a document to tell the user what to do next and then to allow the user to type an entry.

To merge from the keyboard:

- Press the *Merge/Sort* keys, Ctrl-F9.

- Type the name of the primary file, and press Enter.

- Press Enter again to bypass the prompt for the secondary file name. The primary file's text is displayed on the screen, and the cursor is placed at the first {KEYBOARD} code. If you included a {PROMPT} code, the prompt message appears.

- Type the information.

- Press the {END FIELD} key, F9, to continue to the next {KEYBOARD} code.

This type of merge creates one customized letter. To create another letter, simply repeat the procedure.

Follow these steps at your computer to update a memo using the special Merge codes and create the document shown in Figure 10.6.

Figure 10.6   **Primary file MYKMERGE.LRN with Merge codes**

```
{DATE}


{PROMPT}TYPE THE INSIDE ADDRESS-PRESS F9~{KEYBOARD}

Dear {KEYBOARD}:

Enclosed please find my report on the developments at Macco
Plastics for the first quarter of this year.  As you will see, it
has been a dynamic quarter for all phases of Macco's operations.

We look forward to seeing you at the next regional managers'
conference in {KEYBOARD}. In the meantime, keep up the good work.

Sincerely,


Morgan D. Hamilton, President
Macco Plastics, Inc.
```

1. Retrieve the document KMERGE.LRN.

2. Examine the {DATE} code. This code inserts your computer's system date.

3. Examine the {KEYBOARD} codes. The merge stops at each one to allow for typing.

4. Move to the blank line immediately above the *D* in *Dear* in the salutation.

5. Press **Shift-F9** to merge codes, and choose **6 M**ore. The list of merge commands appears in the upper-right corner of the screen.

6. Press ↓ to scroll down the list of commands.

7. Highlight the command *{PROMPT}message~,* and press **Enter** to choose it. WordPerfect prompts

   Enter Message:

8. Enter the following:

   TYPE THE INSIDE ADDRESS-PRESS F9

and press **Enter** to insert the prompt into the typing area.

9. Press **Shift-F9**, and choose **6 M**ore.

10. Press ↑ to scroll upward through the list of commands (or press **K** to jump right to **K**eyboard).

11. Highlight *{KEYBOARD},* and press **Enter** to insert the code.

12. Press **Enter** to end the line.

13. Exit the document, renaming it MYKMERGE.LRN.

14. Press **Ctrl-F9** (Merge/Sort), and choose **1 M**erge to merge information from the keyboard into the completed primary file. WordPerfect prompts you to enter the name of the primary file:

```
Primary file:
```

15. Type **mykmerge.lrn** and press **Enter**. WordPerfect prompts

```
Secondary file:
```

16. Press **Enter** to bypass the secondary-file prompt and perform the merge from the keyboard. Notice the message:

```
* Merging *
```

When WordPerfect gets to the {PROMPT} Merge code, it displays the message you entered in Step 8:

```
TYPE THE INSIDE ADDRESS-PRESS F9
```

in the lower-left corner of your screen.

17. Type **Dave Schmidt** and press **Enter**.

18. Type **4630 Lindell Blvd**. and press **Enter**.

19. Type **St. Louis, MO 63108**. Do *not* press Enter.

20. Press **F9** to end the field and advance the cursor to the next {KEYBOARD} code.

21. Type **Dave** and press **F9** to advance to the next {KEYBOARD} code.

22. Type **August** and press **F9** to complete the letter.

23. Save the document as MYMRGLTR.LRN.

24. Print the document, selecting the Full Document option from the Print menu. Compare your printout to Figure 10.1 near the beginning of this chapter.

25. Clear the typing area by pressing **F7**. Do *not* save the file again.

Here's a helpful hint: When merging from the keyboard, press F9 instead of Enter after typing information unless it should appear on more than one line, such as an address.

CHAPTER SUMMARY

In this chapter, you have learned to use WordPerfect's Merge feature to create and print primary and secondary files and to merge them into one complete form letter.

Here's a quick technique reference for Chapter 10:

Feature or Action	How to Do It
Enter a Field code	**Shift-F9** (Merge), **1** Field, <Field number>, **Enter**
Insert an {END FIELD} code	**F9** (after typing each field)
End the record	**Shift-F9** (Merge), **2** End Record
Merge documents	**Ctrl-F9** (Merge/Sort), **1** Merge, <name of primary file>, **Enter**, <name of secondary file>, **Enter**
Insert a {KEYBOARD} code in a primary file	**Shift-F9** (Merge Codes), **6** More, highlight {KEYBOARD}, **Enter**, <message>, **Enter**

In the next chapter, you will use some of the techniques you have learned in this chapter to create forms and mailing labels.

CHAPTER ELEVEN: FORMS AND LABELS

Creating and Filling
In Forms

Creating Labels

U sing forms at your computer, whether you design them or fill them out, can be quite a challenge. For example, getting the text to print in a certain place can take much planning but still result in error and aggravation.

In this chapter, you will learn about some WordPerfect features that make designing and using forms faster and easier. You'll also use some multi-merge skills that you learned in the previous chapter to create mailing labels.

When you are finished with this chapter, you will be able to:

- Use Line Draw to generate a form

- Use the Advance and Comments commands to prepare a form

- Create mailing labels

CREATING AND FILLING IN FORMS

Everyone has had experience with forms, from job applications to product registration cards. A form is a structure for acquiring and organizing diverse data from many sources. Like a table, a form consists of horizontal and vertical lines, which are often solid. Unlike a table, a form has a structure that can be asymmetrical and irregular, closely matching the diverse kinds of data it must contain.

WordPerfect has several features that can help you design a form and fill it in. Figure 11.1 shows the completed form you will create in this chapter; Figure 11.2 shows the text to be inserted into the form.

 THE LINE DRAW FEATURE

WordPerfect's *Line Draw* feature enables you to use arrow keys to draw boxes, borders, and even simple illustrations, in a variety of line patterns. You can use this feature to draw boxes around text and make forms.

Using Line Draw to Draw Borders
To use the Line Draw feature:

- Press the Screen keys, Ctrl-F3.

- Choose 2 Line Draw. Table 11.1 lists the Line Draw menu options.

- Type the number of the desired option

- Use any arrow key to draw. The cursor appears between small arrows.

- Leave the Line Draw menu by pressing the Cancel key, F1, or the Exit key, F7.

Figure 11.1   **Form layout**

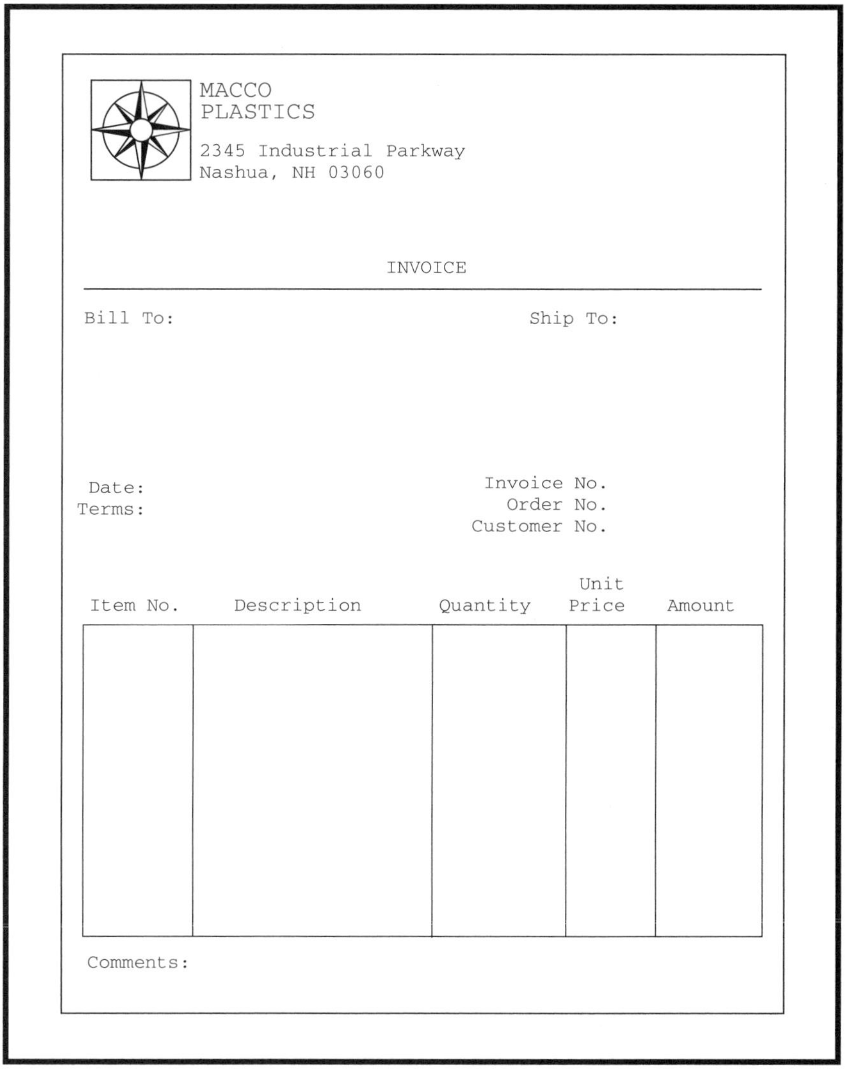

```
            MACCO
            PLASTICS
            2345 Industrial Parkway
            Nashua, NH 03060


                         INVOICE

    Bill To:                        Ship To:




    Date:                      Invoice No.
    Terms:                       Order No.
                              Customer No.


                                        Unit
    Item No.   Description   Quantity    Price    Amount




    Comments:
```

Line Draw can be used to draw around text. However, any text in its path is replaced with the line.

To erase a line, type *5* while in the Line Draw menu, and move the arrow along the unwanted line. As you move the cursor, lines are erased. As with other Line Draw menu choices, you continue to erase until you select another option.

Figure 11.2   **Text to be inserted into the form**

Macco Plastics, Inc.   Atlanta Office
2345 Industrial Parkway   367 Randwich Rd.
Nashua, NH 03060   Atlanta, GA 36301

(today's date)   16051
Net 30   4536
                                                             A067

1   Box sealing tape   5   .91   4.55
2   Paper clips   10   1.25   12.50

Table 11.1   **Line Draw Menu Options**

Number/ Option	Result
1 I	Moving the cursor with an arrow key draws a continuous single line in the direction of the arrow.
2 II	Moving the cursor with an arrow key draws a continuous double line in the direction of the arrow.
3 *	Moving the cursor with an arrow key draws with an asterisk.
4 Change	Displays a menu with eight line patterns. The Other option allows you to draw with a character of your choice: type the selected character number, then use the arrow keys to draw with it.
5 Erase	Moving the cursor erases Line Draw characters in the direction of the arrow.
6 Move	Allows you to move the cursor without disturbing characters and lines on the screen.

Note: Your printer may not be able to print the particular Line Draw character you are using. Read your printer manual if you are in doubt.

Follow these steps at your computer:

1. Retrieve the document FORM.LRN from your Data Disk.

2. Press **PgDn** to move the cursor to the bottom of the page.

3. Position the cursor on the right arrow where the line for the lower border ends (Line 8.51", Position 3.5" on most computers).

4. Press the Screen keys, **Ctrl-F3**.

5. Choose **2** Line Draw to display the Line Draw menu.

6. Choose **1** to draw using a single line.

7. Press → to draw the line, and continue pressing until you arrive at the point where the bottom horizontal line stops (Position 4.2" on most computers).

8. Press ↑ until you reach the connecting line. The box around the Description column is now complete.

Erasing with the Cursor

You may have noticed the misplaced vertical line in the *Quantity* area of your document. To erase it, follow these steps at your computer:

1. Choose **6** Move to move the cursor without drawing or affecting lines.

2. Move to the bottom of the misplaced vertical line under *Quantity* (Line 8.51", Position 4.6" on most computers).

3. Choose **5** Erase.

4. Press ↑ until the line is erased. Stop at the horizontal line at the top of the chart (Line 5.51" on most computers).

5. Choose **6** Move.

6. Move to the incomplete vertical line between the *Quantity* and *Unit Price* columns (Line 6.85", Position 5.2" on most computers). Complete the rest of the chart in Practice Your Skills.

PRACTICE YOUR SKILLS

1. Using Line Draw, complete the form as shown in Figure 11.3.

2. Press **F7** to leave Line Draw.

3. Save the document, renaming it MYFORM.LRN.

Line Draw works in Typeover mode. If, after creating a drawing, you attempt to enter text while in Insert mode, the line characters will be pushed to the right to make room for the text. Press Insert (Ins) to enter Typeover mode before typing text in the Line Draw area.

Figure 11.3   **Completed form**

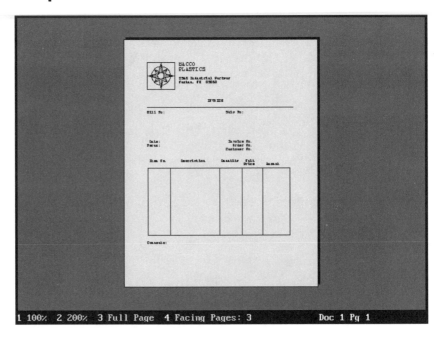

 USING COMMENT AND ADVANCE TO PREPARE THE FORM

To simplify filling in forms at the computer, WordPerfect provides the *Comment* and *Advance* features.

• *Comment* enables you to type notes to yourself or another user; these notes are displayed on the screen but are not printed with the form.

- *Advance* lets you move the print position up, down, left, or right a specific distance from the cursor or the edge of the form.

Creating a Comment

The Comment feature is used to insert notes or reminders that display on the screen but do not print.

To create a comment, follow these steps:

- Press Ctrl-F5 (Text In/Out).

- Choose 4 Comment and 1 Create, then type a note or reminder.

- Press F7 to save the comment and return to the document.

A Comment code appears in the Reveal Codes area, but the View Document option on the Print menu does not display it.

To edit a comment:

- Position the cursor after the Comment code.

- Press the Text In/Out keys, Ctrl-F5.

- Choose Edit. WordPerfect searches backward (toward the beginning of the document) for a Comment code and displays the first one it finds.

- Make any necessary changes.

- Press F7 to save the changes and return to the document. To delete a comment, delete its code from the Reveal Codes area. See Chapter 4 for instructions on viewing and deleting codes.

Display Document Comments must be set to *Yes* to see comments on the screen. Follow these steps to display comments:

- Press Shift-F1 to display the Setup menu.

- Choose 2 - Display and 6 - Edit-Screen Options.

- Choose 2 - Comments Display and select Y for yes.

- Press F7 to save the comment and return to the document.

Now clear the typing area and follow these steps at your computer:

1. Press **Ctrl-F5** (Text In/Out).

2. Choose **4 C**omment to display the Comment menu, and choose **1 C**reate. The Document comment box appears.

3. Type **Bill To:** and press **Enter**.

4. Type the following text:

   ```
   Type the name and address of the company being
   billed.
   ```

   and press **Enter**.

5. Now type the second line of the comment:

   ```
   Note: Press Enter after typing each line.
   ```

6. Press **F7**. The comment appears on the screen in a double-lined box, as shown in Figure 11.4, but will not appear when the form is printed.

7. Display the Reveal Codes area and examine the code:

   ```
   [Comment]
   ```

8. Hide the Reveal Codes area and return to the typing area.

You are allowed to type up to 1,024 characters in a comment box (probably more than you'll ever need). You can also enhance text by applying bold, underlining, and centering.

Entering Advance Commands

The Advance feature is used to print text exactly where you need it on a page. This is very useful when filling in forms. Display the Format menu, Shift-F8, choose Other, then choose Advance. A menu displays directions: *Up, Down, Line, Left, Right,* and *Position.*

- Choose Line or Position when measuring from the top or left of the form.

- Choose Up, Down, Left, or Right to measure from the cursor position, rather than from the edge of the paper.

A code appears in the Reveal Codes area, and any text after the code is advanced to the specified position. The new position is invisible in the typing area, but when the form is filled in, you can see text positions by using View Document (Shift-F7).

Follow these steps at your computer:

1. Display the Format menu by pressing **Shift-F8**.

2. Choose **4 - O**ther and **1 - A**dvance to display the Advance menu.

3. Choose **3 Line**. WordPerfect displays the default:

   ```
   Adv. to line 1"
   ```

Figure 11.4   **Completed comment**

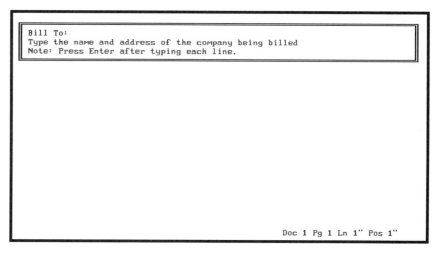

```
Bill To:
Type the name and address of the company being billed
Note: Press Enter after typing each line.




                                                    Doc 1 Pg 1 Ln 1" Pos 1"
```

4. Type **3.25** to set the Advance position to 3.25", and press **Enter**.

5. Choose **1 - A**dvance and **6 P**osition. WordPerfect displays the default:

Adv. to pos 1"

6. Press **Enter** to accept the default position.

7. Press **F7** to return to the typing area.

8. Display the Reveal Codes area, and examine the codes

[AdvToLn:3.25"][AdvToPos:1"]

9. Hide the Reveal Codes area, and return to the typing area.

10. Save the document, renaming it MYTFORM.LRN (for MY Test FORM).

Typing Information in the Form

To enter text in a form, clear the typing area and follow these steps at your computer:

1. Retrieve the document INVOICE.LRN.

2. Position the cursor on the blank line immediately under the Date comment box (Line 4.34", Position 1.7" on most computers).

3. Press **Shift-F5** (Date/Outline), and choose **1** Date **T**ext to insert today's date.

4. Press ↓ to move under the *Terms* comment box.

5. Type **Net 30** and press ↓ to move under the *Invoice No* comment box.

6. Type **16051** and press ↓ to move under *Order No.*

7. Type **4536** and press ↓ to move under *Customer No.*

8. Type **A067** (the customer number), and press ↓ twice to move to the *Item No.* field.

9. Type **2** (the item number), and tab to the *Description* field.

10. Type **Paper clips** (the description), and tab to the *Quantity* field.

11. Type **10** (the quantity), and tab to the *Unit Price* field.

12. Type **1.25** (the unit price), and tab to the *Amount* field.

13. Type **12.50** (the amount), and press **Enter** to move to the next line.

14. Save the document as MYINVOIC.LRN.

15. Go to the View Document area (Shift-F7) to view the completed form. Figure 11.5 shows the form in the View Document area.

16. Press **F7** to leave the View Document area.

17. From the Print menu, select **1 - F**ull Document to print the form.

18. Press **F7** to clear the typing area.

CREATING LABELS

In Chapter 10, you learned how to use WordPerfect's mail-merge feature to create customized letters. You use mail-merge to create mailing labels by extracting names and addresses contained in a secondary file and printing them on mailing labels.

When printing on anything other than standard 8½" by 11" paper, WordPerfect needs to know the size, shape, and type of paper to print correctly. This information is stored in a *printer definition*. To print labels, you must adjust the printer definition accordingly. Then, when the printer definition is activated, it tells the printer how to print the labels.

Figure 11.5   **Form with inserted text**

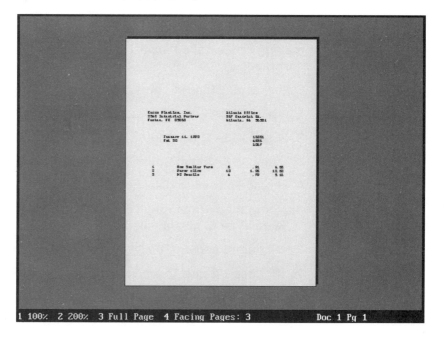

 CREATING A LABEL DEFINITION

The first thing you need to do is create a printer definition for labels. With the typing area cleared, follow these steps at your computer:

1. Display the Format menu by pressing **Shift-F8**.

2. Choose **2 - P**age to display the Page menu.

3. Choose **7 - P**aper **S**ize/Type to display the Paper Size/Type menu.

4. Choose **2 A**dd to display the Paper Type menu.

5. Choose **4 - L**abels to display the Edit Paper Definition menu.

6. Choose **8 - L**abels and type **Y** to display the Labels menu. The default settings for label size, number of columns and rows, and distance between labels are displayed.

7. Change the settings to match the labels you are using, or press **F7** to accept the default settings, three labels across.

8. Press **F7** three more times to return to the typing area.

ACTIVATING THE PRINTER DEFINITION FOR LABELS

The second step in creating labels is to activate the printer definition you just created. To do this, you will customize the default formatting codes, called *initial codes*, that WordPerfect attaches to this document.

Follow these steps at your computer:

1. Display the Format menu by pressing **Shift-F8**.

2. Choose **3 - D**ocument to display the Document menu.

3. Choose **2 - Initial C**odes.

4. Press **Shift-F8** to display the Format menu again.

5. From the Format menu choose **2 - P**age, and choose **7 - Paper Size/Type** to display the Paper Size/Type menu.

6. Highlight *Labels*. The label definition reads *3 X 10*.

7. Choose **1 S**elect to activate the definition.

8. Press **F7** three times to return to the typing area.

USING MERGE TO CREATE THE PRIMARY FILE

The third step in creating labels is to decide which fields you want printed from the secondary file and then to create the primary file. Our primary file uses six fields: first name; last name; street address; city; state; and zip code. It will look like this:

```
{FIELD}1~ {FIELD}2~
{FIELD}4~
{FIELD}5~, {FIELD}6~  {FIELD}7~
```

Follow these steps at your computer:

1. Press the Merge Code keys, **Shift-F9**, and choose **1 F**ield. WordPerfect prompts

   ```
   Enter Field:
   ```

2. Type **1** and press **Enter**.

3. Press **Spacebar**.

4. Press **Shift-F9**, and choose **1 F**ield. WordPerfect prompts

   ```
   Enter Field:
   ```

5. Type **2** and press **Enter**.

6. Insert the remaining field codes, as shown above, to complete the primary file.

7. Save the document as MYLABEL.LRN, but remain in WordPerfect.

 MERGING THE LABELS

The last step in creating labels is to merge the primary and secondary files to create the final mailing labels. Follow these steps at your computer:

1. Press **Ctrl-F9** (Merge/Sort) and choose **1 M**erge. WordPerfect prompts you to identify the primary file's name:

   `Primary file:`

2. Type **mylabel.lrn** and press **Enter**. Now WordPerfect prompts

   `Secondary file:`

3. Type **xmyadlis.lrn** and press **Enter**. The labels are merged.

4. Compare your document to the one shown in Figure 11.6.

5. View the document. The labels appear three across.

6. Return to the typing area.

7. Exit the document without saving your changes.

CHAPTER SUMMARY

In this chapter, you have learned how to create forms using the Line Draw, Comment, and Advance features. You've also learned how to use mail-merge to create mailing labels.

Here's a quick technique reference for Chapter 11:

Feature or Action	How to Do It
Line Draw	**Ctrl-F3** (Screen), **2 L**ine Draw, option number of the Line Draw character, use the arrow keys to draw
Move the cursor in Line Draw without drawing	**6 M**ove

Feature or Action	How to Do It
Erase lines in Line Draw	**5 E**rase
Create a comment	**Ctrl-F5** (Text In/Out), **4 C**omment, **1 C**reate, type the comment, **F7**
Advance text on a page	**Shift-F8** (Format), **4 - O**ther, **1 - A**dvance, either **1 U**p, **2 D**own, **3 L**ine, **4 L**eft, **5 R**ight, or **6 P**osition, type a measurement, **Enter, F7**
Create a label definition	**Shift-F8** (Format), **2 P**age, **7 - P**aper Size/Type, **2 A**dd, **4 - L**abels, **8 - L**abels, **Y, F7**
Activate printer definition for labels	**Shift-F8** (Format), **2 - P**age, **7 - P**aper Size/Type, highlight *Labels*, **1 S**elect, **F7**

In the next chapter, you will learn how to import and edit graphics in your document. You'll also learn some advanced printing techniques.

Figure 11.6   **Merged labels**

```
        Marlene Albert
        1135 College Avenue
        Topeka, KS  66604
        ===============================================
        Janice Alexander
        2745 Church St.
        Seattle, WA  97220
        ===============================================
        Dorothy Anderson
        250 Main St.
        Boston, MA  48189
        ===============================================
        Marvin Bean
        1582 Emmett St.
        Los Angeles, CA  92001
        ===============================================
        Clair Cooper
        60 East Ave.
        Reno, NV  89502
        ===============================================
        William Davis
        354 Pinewood Rd.
        White Plains, NY  10605
        ===============================================
        Joyce Farrell
        4865 West Century Blvd.
        Inglewood, CA  90304
        ===============================================
        Amy Fitzgerald
        121 Holiday Square
        Topeka, KS  66607
        ===============================================
```

CHAPTER TWELVE: GRAPHICS

Importing a
Graphic

Editing a Graphic
Image

Additional Printing
Techniques

You've seen many of the ways that WordPerfect enables you to create and manipulate text in your document. The program also provides you with a powerful tool for incorporating graphic images, or *graphics*, into your documents. In this chapter, you will learn how to incorporate and edit graphics in your document. You'll also learn some advanced printing techniques that give you better control over the printing process.

There are a couple of important reasons for adding graphics to a document:

- To illustrate material covered in the text. For example, suppose you have written a detailed analysis of the rise in world population in the twentieth century. Illustrating your findings with bar charts or graphs might help your readers grasp the information at a glance.

- To enhance the appearance of the document, since a document with graphics looks more professional. Figure 12.1 shows a newsletter containing an illustration that adds much to the overall look of the document.

When done with this chapter, you will be able to:

- Incorporate a graphic into your document

- Move, size, and rotate a graphic

- Add a caption to your graphic

- Print selected pages of a document

- Cancel, rush, and display print jobs

IMPORTING A GRAPHIC

You can place graphics in any WordPerfect document, as well as in headers and footers. Images can be *imported* into a WordPerfect document from many draw or paint software programs or from sources of digitized images (clip art). (For a list of the graphic programs WordPerfect supports, see the Graphic Images section in the appendix of the WordPerfect manual.) WordPerfect 5.1 also comes with a number of graphics files (denoted by the .WPG extension in the file name), which you can use in your documents and edit.

WordPerfect cannot create graphics; however, once you load an image into WordPerfect, you can size it, move it, and rotate it. There is no limit to the number of graphics in a document. However, adding graphics is like adding text—the document's pagination adjusts automatically. The more graphics you add to the document, the more you must adjust the rest of the document. And the more graphics a document contains, the larger the file becomes; it can even fill an entire disk and, therefore, require that you divide the file into smaller files. Even small files with graphics can take a long time to print.

Figure 12.1   **Sample document with graphic**

All the News
Worth Printing

MACCO
NEWS

A Quarterly Publication from Macco Plastics, Inc.

Vol. II No. 5   Macco Plastics, Inc.   First Quarter

Production and Sales Update

The first quarter of this year has seen an unbelievable increase in sales for all of Macco's regional sales offices. Most of this is due to a rebound in the general economy, as well as in the particular industries that Macco serves. Particularly strong were the automobile segment and sales to consumer goods manufacturers. Included in this report are tables showing the breakdown in sales by industry.

Altogether, it has been an exciting quarter for all of us at Macco. You, as regional managers, can be proud of the job you and your people have done in making Macco the leader in plastic technologies.

Personnel Update

New Positions

We are again looking for new people to fill several key positions here at headquarters, as well as some regional management positions. Most of these positions are new, but some have opened up as a result of retirements.

Retirements

Mark Short, sales coordinator in the Atlanta office, has recently retired after twenty years with Macco. Marlene Albert, training administrator here at headquarters, has retired after fifteen years with the company. We will all miss Mark and Marlene, and wish them the best in their retirement.

Available Positions

Consult the second quarter newsletter for a list of available positions, offices, and dates these positions must be filled.

1

Figure 12.1 (continued)

Production Update

Production Changes

As part of the overall restructuring announced last year, we are streamlining our production systems. Two new products, which will be announced next quarter, will be produced in Nashville.

Production News

Computer-Controlled Manufacturing

The Nashville group has been running a computer-controlled manufacturing line. Later this year, assuming all goes well, they will scale up the system to handle the entire plant.

Companywide Computerization

Dave Schmidt will be in charge of computer-controlled manufacturing project as it affects companywide operations. He will be contacting you and the appropriate people on your staffs to schedule evaluations, vendor coordination, and staff resource planning for this project.

Sales Results

As we mentioned earlier, overall sales increased in almost all of Macco's product lines. Particularly strong were sales to consumer goods manufacturers and automobile manufacturers.

Overall, as you can see, it has been an impressive quarter of growth and change here at Macco. You should be proud of what you've done. Let's keep up the good work!

2

It's important to remember that you will only be able to print graphics if your printer has graphics capabilities. Also, to view graphics on your screen, your computer must be equipped with a graphics display card.

To import a graphic into a document, you need to:

- Create and define a graphics box in a WordPerfect document
- Copy the file with the image into the box

 CREATING A FIGURE BOX

The first step in importing a graphic is to create a *graphics box* to hold the image. Each box you create is automatically assigned a number. In the Reveal Codes area, the box is represented by a code, which displays the box type and number. A graphics box can contain an image or text, or it can remain empty.

There are five types of graphics boxes. Each box type is numbered separately. You can put any graphic in any type of box, but Word-Perfect suggests using the five types as follows:

- *Figure* boxes for images, diagrams, and charts
- *Table* boxes for maps, statistical data, and tables of numbers
- *Text* boxes for quotations or other text that you want to set off from the rest of the document
- *Equation* boxes for mathematical and scientific equations
- *User-defined* boxes for any image or document that doesn't fit into the above categories

To create and define a graphics box:

- Position the cursor where you want to place the graphics box.
- Press the Graphics keys, Alt-F9.
- Select a box type (for example, 1 Figure).
- Choose 1 Create, and define the box's characteristics: its caption, vertical and horizontal positions, size, and whether text is to wrap around it or print over it.
- Press F7 to return to the document.

Follow these steps at your computer:

1. Retrieve the file CHAP12.LRN from the Data Disk.
2. Move the cursor to the top of the document, if it's not already there.

3. Press the Graphics keys, **Alt-F9** (Graphics), to display the Graphics menu.

4. Choose **1 F**igure, and choose **1 C**reate to display the Definition Figure menu.

5. Choose **6 - H**orizontal Position. The Horizontal Position menu appears at the bottom of the screen.

6. Choose **1 L**eft.

7. Choose **7 - S**ize, and choose **3** Set **B**oth to assign the width and the height dimensions. WordPerfect displays the default width:

   `Width = 3.25"`

   If you set either width or height alone, WordPerfect automatically calculates the other dimension to retain the original proportion of the box. Choosing 3 Set Both allows you to enter both dimensions.

8. Type **1.5** and press **Enter** to assign the new width value. Word-Perfect displays the default height:

   `Height = 3.25"`

9. Type **1.4** and press **Enter** to assign the new height value.

10. Press **F7** to return to the typing area.

11. Display the Reveal Codes area, and examine the code:

    `[Fig Box:1;;]`

    When a graphics file is incorporated into the figure box, the graphics' file name is automatically inserted between the two semicolons in the code.

12. Hide the Reveal Codes area to return to the typing area.

13. Use View Document to view the document, as shown in Figure 12.2. Observe that text has wrapped around the empty box.

14. Return to the typing area.

To change the characteristics of a graphics box that you have already defined:

- Position the cursor where you want to place the graphics box.

- Press the Graphics keys, Alt-F9.

- Select a box type (for example, 1 Figure).

Figure 12.2   **Figure box**

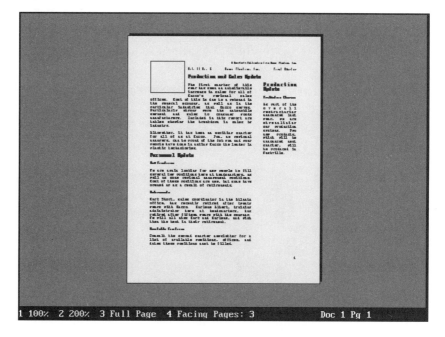

- Choose 2 Edit, type the number of the graphics box, and press Enter. Use the menu to change the box's characteristics.

PREPARING THE DOCUMENT FOR THE GRAPHIC

Right now, you can see that text wraps around the figure box. To make the graphic stand out, you can move the text under the graphic. The document also needs a heading. Follow the steps below to remedy these problems.

1. With the cursor positioned under the *A* in *A Quarterly*, press **Enter** five times to end the line and insert four blank lines.

2. Press ↑ to move up to a blank line.

3. Press **Alt-F6** to move to the right margin.

4. Display the Font menu, and choose **1 S**ize, then **7 E**xt Large.

5. Type **MACCO** and press **Enter**.

6. Press **Alt-F6**, type **NEWS**, and press **Enter** to end the line.

7. Press → to turn off Extra Large font by moving the cursor beyond the Extra Large code.

8. Press **Enter** four times to end the line and insert three blank lines.

9. Use View Document to examine the text below the graphic, as shown in Figure 12.3.

10. Return to the typing area.

Figure 12.3   **Text repositioned**

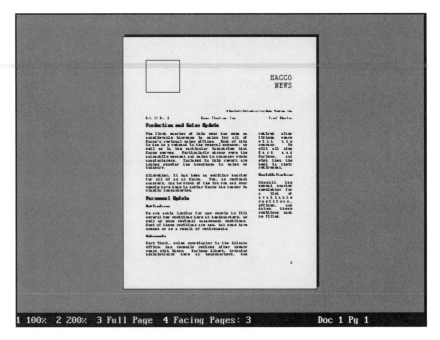

IMPORTING A GRAPHIC INTO A FIGURE BOX

To retrieve an image into a graphics box:

• Press the Graphics keys, Alt-F9.

• Select the box type.

• Choose 2 Edit. Type the number of the box, and press Enter.

• Choose 1 - Filename.

- Type the name of the graphics file, and press Enter.
- Press Exit, F7, to return to the document.

Make sure the Data Disk is in drive A, and follow these steps at your computer:

1. Press the Graphics keys, **Alt-F9**, to display the Graphics menu.

2. Choose **1 F**igure, and then choose **2 E**dit. WordPerfect displays the default number of the figure box to be edited.

   Figure number? 2

   2 is the default, even though there is only one figure box.

3. Type **1** and press **Enter** to display the Definition Figure menu.

4. Choose **1 - Filename**. WordPerfect prompts you to tell it where to find the graphics file, including the file's directory:

   Enter filename:

5. Type **a:\announce.wpg** and press **Enter**.

6. Press **F7** to return to the typing area.

7. Use View Document to observe the image in the figure box, as shown in Figure 12.4. You can increase the viewing size to get a better look at the image.

8. Return to the typing area.

EDITING A GRAPHIC IMAGE

To change the content of the image, you must edit it in the program in which it was created. In WordPerfect you can change its location, size, scale, and rotation, using the Graphics Editor. You can also add a caption to explain an image or tie it into your text.

MOVING, SCALING, AND ROTATING A GRAPHIC IMAGE

When you move an image in the Graphics Editor, you move the image within the graphics box; the box itself does not move. Likewise, when you scale a graphic, you change the size of the graphic image, not of the box. (Enlarging the scale means magnifying the image within the figure box.) And when you rotate a graphic, you change the angle of its display within the box; the box does not change.

Figure 12.4   **Figure box with graphic**

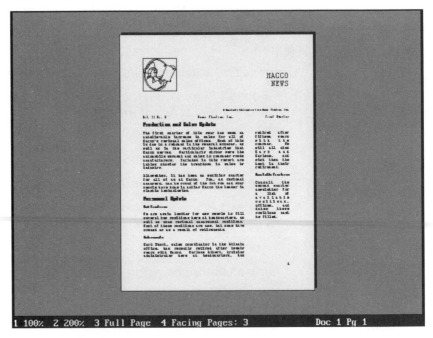

You can also change the location of a graphics box on the page and the location of the image in the box by following these steps:

- Press the Graphics keys, Alt-F9, to display the Graphics menu.

- Choose the box type.

- Choose 2 Edit, and enter the number of the box.

- From the Definition Figure menu, choose 5 - Vertical Position or 6 - Horizontal Position.

  - If you chose 5 - Vertical Position, the following message appears:

    `Offset from top of paragraph: 0"`

    The inch measurement refers to the current distance of the cursor from the top of the paragraph. It tells you how far the top of the box will be from the top of the paragraph. 0" indicates that the cursor is on the top line of the paragraph. Pressing Enter places the top of the box at the top of the paragraph; typing the number of inches and pressing Enter places the top of the box that distance from the top of the paragraph.

- If you chose 6 - Horizontal Position, choose 1 Left to left-align the box, 2 Right to right-align it, 3 Center, or 4 Full to spread the figure between the left and right margins.

- Press Exit, F7, to leave the Graphics Editor.

To move, scale, or rotate a graphic image within its box, follow these steps:

- Press the Graphics keys, Alt-F9.

- Choose the appropriate box type, and choose 2 Edit. Enter the number of the box.

- From the Definition Figure menu, choose 9 Edit. The graphic is then displayed in the Graphics Editor screen.

- Make your changes as described below, and press Exit (F7) to leave the Graphics Editor.

In the Graphics Editor screen, there are two ways to make changes:

- You can adjust the image by keystroke: Use the arrow keys to move the image within the box; use PgUp or PgDn to increase or decrease the size of the image; use the plus and minus keys to rotate the image. The extent by which these keys move, scale, or rotate the image depends on the percentage displayed in the bottom-right corner of the screen. Press Ins to change the default percentage of 10% to 1%, 5%, or 25%.

- You can also adjust the image by selecting Move, Scale, or Rotate from the menu, and typing the amount of change that you want, in inches. For example, if you want to move the image:

  - Choose 1 Move.

  - Type the horizontal distance you want to move, in inches. Type a negative number to move the image to the left or a positive number to move it to the right.

  - Press Enter.

  - Type the vertical distance you want to move. Type a positive number to move the image up or a negative number to move it down.

  - Press Enter.

As you can see, you actually have more control using the menu.

Follow these steps at your computer:

1. Press **Alt-F9** to display the Graphics menu.

2. Choose **1 F**igure, and choose **2 E**dit. You can see the prompt

   Figure number? 2

3. Type **1** and press **Enter** to display the Definition Figure menu.

4. From the Definition Figure menu, choose **9 - E**dit. The image appears on your screen. The percentage is displayed in the bottom-right corner of the screen (10%).

5. Press **Ins** three times. Examine the percentage (25%).

6. Press **PgUp** three times. Notice that the size of the image has increased.

7. Press **Ins**, and notice that the percentage has changed to 10%.

8. Press **+** to rotate the graphic. Confirm that the image has rotated by comparing your screen to the one shown in Figure 12.5.

9. Press **F7** to return to the Definition Figure menu.

 ## ADDING A CAPTION TO A GRAPHIC

You might want to add captions to an illustration to help the reader understand it. In WordPerfect, not only can you create the text for the caption, but you can also format it in any way.

The caption can be as long as you want; it will wrap according to the width of the graphics box.

To add a caption to a graphic:

- Press Alt-F9 (Graphics).

- Choose 1 Figure to display the Definition Figure menu.

- Choose 3 Caption.

- If you wish, edit or erase the default caption (for example, *Figure 1*) and type the new caption.

- Press Exit, F7, to return to the typing area.

Figure 12.5 **Scaled and rotated graphic**

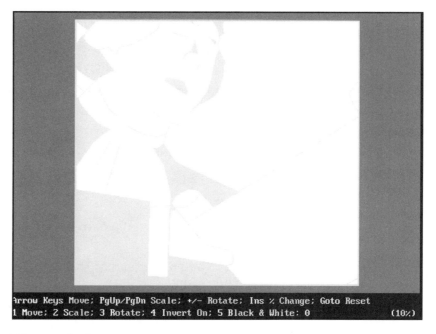

```
Arrow Keys Move; PgUp/PgDn Scale; +/- Rotate; Ins % Change; Goto Reset
1 Move; 2 Scale; 3 Rotate; 4 Invert On; 5 Black & White; 0          (10%)
```

With the Definition Figure menu displayed, follow these steps at your computer:

1. Choose **3 - C**aption.

2. Press **Backspace** to erase the default caption *Figure 1*.

3. Type **All the News Worth Printing**.

4. Press **F7** as instructed on the screen, to return to the Definition Figure menu.

5. Press **F7** once again to return to the typing area.

6. Use View Document to observe the edited graphic in the graphics box. Set the view option to **1** (100%).

 ADJUSTING PAGINATION

Adding a graphic to your document is much like adding text—both take up space. This means that the graphic must push text forward and take its place. That's why adding a graphic sometimes affects pagination. After you've added your graphic, it's a good idea to examine the document in the View Document area to see whether the pages break where you want.

Follow these steps while still in the View Document area:

1. Set the View Document option to **3** (Full Page).

2. Move to and examine pages 2 and 3. How has adding graphics affected pagination?

3. Display page 3 on the screen.

4. Return to the typing area.

5. Press **Shift-F2** (Search Backward). WordPerfect prompts

   `<- Srch:`

6. Press **Ctrl-Enter** to insert a hard page break ([HPg] code) into the search field.

7. Press **F2** to begin the search. The cursor advances to the first [HPg] code found.

8. Press **Backspace** to delete the [HPg] code between pages 2 and 3.

9. Using View Document, observe that the newsletter now has two pages.

10. Display page 1.

11. Press **Spacebar** to return to the Print menu.

12. Choose **2 - Page** to print page 1. Compare your printout to the first page of the document shown in Figure 12.1.

13. Exit the document, renaming it MYCHAP12.LRN.

ADDITIONAL PRINTING TECHNIQUES

Now that you are creating longer and more complex documents that take advantage of many different WordPerfect features, you are probably printing your documents more often just to make sure they look right. You may find that you're wasting a lot of paper by printing draft copies. You may also find that printing pages with graphics can take a long time. WordPerfect offers you printing options to help you take better control of the printing process while saving you time and paper.

In Chapter 1, you learned how to print a full document. You also learned that WordPerfect allows you to print in the background, so that while printing you can continue to edit the same or another document or even create a new one. No doubt you will often want to print a full document. Sometimes, however, you will want to print only a page or selected pages. And at times you will want to control the flow of information to your printer—to rush or cancel a print job, for example.

 PRINTING SELECTED PAGES OF A DOCUMENT

When a document is in the typing area, you can choose 1 - Full Document from the Print menu (Shift-F7), shown in Figure 12.6, to print the entire document or 2 - Page to print the page on which you have positioned the cursor.

Figure 12.6   **WordPerfect Print menu**

```
Print

        1 - Full Document
        2 - Page
        3 - Document on Disk
        4 - Control Printer
        5 - Multiple Pages
        6 - View Document
        7 - Initialize Printer


Options

        S - Select Printer                    Epson FX-80/100
        B - Binding Offset                    0"
        N - Number of Copies                  1
        U - Multiple Copies Generated by      WordPerfect
        G - Graphics Quality                  Medium
        T - Text Quality                      High




Selection: 0
```

To print selected pages of the document that is in the typing area, choose 5 - Multiple Pages from the Print menu (Shift-F7), and then type the numbers of the pages that you wish to print. Table 12.1 shows you how to enter numbers of selected pages or a range of pages (after choosing 5 - Multiple Pages from the Print menu).

Table 12.1   **Multiple Pages Options**

Type	To Print...
<#>, Enter	Only page #
<#>-, Enter	From page # to the end of the document (for example, *2-, Enter* to print from page 2 to the end)
<#>-<#>, Enter	A range, from the first # to the second # (for example, *2-5* to print pages 2 through 5)
-<#>, Enter	From the beginning of the document to page # (for example, *-5* to print pages 1 through 5)
<#>,<#>, Enter	Only the two pages specified (for example, *2,5* to print pages 2 and 5)

Note: The symbol <#> represents any single page number that you type; for example, page *2*.

CANCELING, RUSHING, AND DISPLAYING PRINT JOBS

Whenever you tell WordPerfect to print a file, it copies it to a new location on disk to create a temporary file, and then prints from that temporary file. This allows you to continue working on the same document that is being printed. Each file or part of a file that you send to the printer is considered a *print job*. Because of the way WordPerfect prints, you can send multiple print jobs to the printer. WordPerfect then uses the print jobs to create a *Job List*, a list of files or parts of files waiting to be printed.

Once you have sent the file to the printer, the Print menu choice 4 - Control Printer (see Figure 12.6) enables you to cancel a print job or rush a job by placing it at the top of the list. You can also stop the printer temporarily to fix a paper jam and restart it. Figure 12.7 shows the Control Printer area. The available Control Printer options are described in Table 12.2.

Figure 12.7   **Control Printer area**

```
Print: Control Printer

Current Job

Job Number: None                          Page Number:   None
Status:     No print jobs                 Current Copy: None
Message:    None
Paper:      None
Location:   None
Action:     None


Job List

Job  Document              Destination        Print Options




Additional Jobs Not Shown: 0



1 Cancel Job(s); 2 Rush Job; 3 Display Jobs; 4 Go (start printer); 5 Stop: 0
```

Table 12.2   **Control Printer Options**

Option	Purpose
1 Cancel Job(s)	To remove any of the documents from the Job List. Enter the job number.
2 Rush Job	To change the priority of a document in the Job List. Enter the job number.
3 Display Jobs	Documents in the Job List are assigned a job number. Normally only three jobs appear in the Job List at once; use this option to display a list of *all* the documents waiting to be printed.
4 Go (start printer)	To restart the printer after you use the Stop option.
5 Stop	To stop the printer *without* cancelling a job. Use stop when you need to change a ribbon or fix a paper jam; use Go to restart the printer.

CHAPTER SUMMARY

In this chapter, you have learned how to incorporate a graphic into a document and to edit the graphic by moving it, changing its scale, and rotating it. You also learned how to specify pages of a document to print and how to control the flow of data to your printer by canceling and rushing print jobs.

Here's a quick technique reference for graphics:

Feature or Action	How to Do It
Create a graphics box	**Alt-F9** (Graphics), select a box type, **1 C**reate, define the box's characteristics, **F7** (Exit)
Set dimensions of the graphics box	**Alt-F9** (Graphics); select the box type; **1 C**reate; **7 - S**ize; **1 S**et Width, **2 S**et Height, or **3** Set **B**oth; enter each dimension
Retrieve an image into the box	**Alt-F9** (Graphics), select the box type, **2 E**dit, **1 -** Filename, type the name of the graphics file or press **F5** to list the graphics files, **Enter, F7** (Exit)
Change the graphic's horizontal position	**Alt-F9** (Graphics); select the box type; **1 C**reate; **6 -** Horizontal Position; **1 L**eft, **2 R**ight, **3 C**enter, or **4 F**ull
Move the image within the box	**Alt-F9** (Graphics), enter the box type, **2 E**dit, **9 E**dit (Graphics Editor), arrow keys (or use the menu)
Increase or decrease image size	**Alt-F9** (Graphics), enter the box type, **2 E**dit, **9 E**dit (Graphics Editor), **PgUp** or **PgDn** (or use the menu)
Rotate the image	**Alt-F9** (Graphics), enter the box type, **2 E**dit, **9 E**dit (Graphics Editor), **+** or **-** (or use the menu)
Change the percentage of image editing	**Alt-F9** (Graphics), enter the box type, **2 E**dit, **9 E**dit (Graphics Editor), **Ins** (each time the key is pressed, the percentage changes to 1%, 5%, 10%, or 25%).

Feature or Action	How to Do It
Add a caption	**Alt-F9** (Graphics), select the box type, **2** Edit, **3 - C**aption, delete the existing caption, type the new caption, **F7** (Exit) *twice*
Search for a [HPg] code	**F2** (Search) or **Shift-F2** (Search Backward), **Ctrl-Enter** (Hard Page)

For a quick technique reference for printing, see Tables 12.1 and 12.2.

In the final chapter of this book, you will learn how to save time and keystrokes for repetitive tasks by creating and using macros.

CHAPTER THIRTEEN: MACROS

Thus far, you have learned how to use a broad range of Word-Perfect features, from the simple to the sophisticated. The simplest ones, such as applying bold, require a single keystroke; the sophisticated ones, such as formatting a document, can require a long series of keystrokes. If you often repeat the same series of keystrokes, then you'll want to learn how to use WordPerfect's Macro feature. It will enable you to assign any series of keystrokes to one or two keys.

A *macro* is a file that stores keystrokes that you must often repeat. By running the macro, you repeat those keystrokes automatically. You can create a macro to display a menu or series of menus; to access any WordPerfect feature; and even to type text automatically, saving you the time of retyping it yourself. When the macro is replayed, every recorded keystroke is repeated in sequence on the screen, just as if you had pressed all the keys yourself.

Macros can lessen the burden of tedious procedures, aid inexperienced users in doing complicated tasks, and automate and standardize procedures. Common macros do such things as closing letters, formatting and printing documents, and setting up headers and footers.

When done with this chapter, you will be able to:

- Create a macro
- Name a macro
- Replay macro keystrokes
- Edit a macro

CREATING A MACRO TO FORMAT A LETTER

Creating a macro is almost as easy as typing the keystrokes you want to record. To create a macro:

- Press the Macro Define keys, Ctrl-F10.
- Type a one- to eight-character name for the macro and press Enter.
- Optionally, type up to 39 characters describing the macro.
- Press Enter. A keystroke recorder is turned on; it records every key you press until you turn the recorder off again. The message

  Macro Def

  flashes on screen while the recorder is active.
- Type the keystrokes you want to record, exactly as you type them while working on a document. If you make a mistake, correct it the same way you normally do.
- Press Ctrl-F10 again to turn the macro recorder off.

Each macro is stored in its own file. WordPerfect appends .WPM, the three-character extension, to macro file names. However, macro files *cannot* be retrieved into the typing area through the Retrieve or List Files features; you will learn how to use your macros later in this chapter.

Try creating a macro that will format a letter. With the typing area cleared, follow these steps at your computer:

1. Press **Ctrl-F10** (Macro Define). WordPerfect prompts you to name the macro:

    ```
    Define macro:
    ```

2. Type **myformat**, the name of your macro file. WordPerfect automatically appends the .WPM extension.

3. Press **Enter**. WordPerfect prompts you to describe the macro, if you want:

    ```
    Description:
    ```

4. Press **Enter** to bypass the optional description. The following flashing message tells you that the keystroke recorder has been turned on:

    ```
    Macro Def
    ```

    This message remains on the screen and the recorder records every keystroke you enter until you turn the recorder off.

5. Display the Line menu by pressing **Shift-F8** and **1 - L**ine.

6. Choose **7 - M**argins.

7. Enter **1.5** to set a left margin of 1.5".

8. Enter **1.5** to set a right margin of 1.5".

9. Press **Enter** to return to the Format menu.

10. Display the Format Page menu (**2 - P**age).

11. Choose **1 - C**enter Page (top to bottom), and type **Y**.

12. Return to the typing area.

TYPING A HEADING FOR THE LETTER MACRO

You can now start typing the information that you want all of your letters to contain. Let's start with the return address. Follow these steps at your computer:

1. Turn on **Caps Lock**.

2. Position the cursor at the center of the line by pressing **Shift-F6**.

3. Turn on **Bold**, and type **MACCO PLASTICS, INC**. The heading is bold and centered.

4. Turn off both **bold** and **Caps Lock**.

5. Press **Enter** to end the line.

PRACTICE YOUR SKILLS

1. Using Figure 13.1 as a guide, type and center the rest of the inside address. Do not insert today's date yet; you will do so in the next activity.

2. After the last line, press **Enter** four times to leave three blank lines.

Figure 13.1 **The macro for letter-opening**

```
                    MACCO PLASTICS, INC.
                   2345 Industrial Parkway
                   Nashua, NH   03060


        (Today's Date)
```

 INSERTING A DATE CODE

Macros automate a fixed sequence of keystrokes. By inserting the date or a pause, you can incorporate information that changes from letter to letter. A date code automatically inserts the current date in your letters any time you run the macro.

Follow these steps at your computer:

1. Press the Date/Outline keys (**Shift-F5**), and choose **2 D**ate **C**ode. The current system date is inserted at the cursor position.

2. Press **Enter** four times to end the line and skip three blank lines.

3. Press **Ctrl-F10** to turn off the keystroke recorder. The flashing prompt disappears from the screen, signaling the end of the macro recording session.

4. Move the cursor to the top of the document.

5. From the Reveal Codes area, examine the codes

   `[L/R Mar:1.5",1.5"][Center Pg][Center][BOLD]`

   When you create a macro, the keystokes you type actually take effect on the current document. You now have a document containing nothing but the keystrokes you just recorded.

6. Hide the Reveal Codes area and return to the typing area.

7. Exit the document *without* saving by pressing **F7** and typing **N** twice. Your macro is still saved as MYFORMAT.WPM.

CREATING A MACRO WITH A PAUSE

A pause inserted in a macro allows you to enter information from the keyboard when you run the macro. For example, you might create a macro to generate the standard parts of a memo, such as the *TO:* and *FROM:* entries. Inserting a pause after *TO:* signals the macro to stop at that point so you can type the name of the person to whom the memo is addressed. Pressing Enter after typing the information signals the macro to continue where it left off.

To insert a pause in a macro:

- As you are recording keystrokes in the macro, press Ctrl-PgUp.

- Choose 1 Pause to temporarily stop the macro. The cursor returns to the typing area.

- Press Enter to break the pause and continue creating the macro.

With the typing area cleared, follow these steps at your computer:

1. Press **Ctrl-F10** (Macro Define). WordPerfect prompts

   `Define macro:`

2. Type **myclose** (the macro file name) and press **Enter**. WordPerfect automatically appends the .WPM extension. WordPerfect then prompts you to describe your macro:

   `Description:`

3. Press **Enter** to bypass the optional description. The following flashing message tells you that the keystroke recorder is on:

   `Macro Def`

4. Press **Enter** to skip a blank line.

5. Type **Sincerely,** and press **Enter** four times to leave ample space for a signature.

6. Press **Ctrl-PgUp** to display the Macro Commands menu:

   `1 Pause; 2 Display; 3 Assign; 4 Comment: 0`

7. Choose **1 P**ause to pause the macro while it is running and allow you to type the name of the person sending the letter.

8. Press **Enter** to break the pause.

9. Press **Enter** to end the line.

10. Press **Ctrl-PgUp** to bring up the Macro Commands menu again.

11. Choose **1 P**ause to pause the macro and allow you to type the title of the letter's author.

12. Press **Enter** to break the pause.

13. Press **Enter** to end the line.

14. Type **Macco Plastics, Inc.** and press **Enter** twice.

15. Type **Enclosure** and press **Enter** twice.

16. Type **cc:** and press **Tab** so that the macro will automatically tab to where the person using the macro should enter the list of *cc* names.

PRACTICE YOUR SKILLS

1. Using Figure 13.2 as a guide, type the names in the cc list. Press **Enter** after the last name in the list.

2. Press **Ctrl-F10** to end the macro recording session.

3. Exit the document without saving. The macro remains saved on disk.

A helpful hint: Macros can be deleted or renamed in WordPerfect's List Files area or in DOS. If you should ever decide to rename a macro file, be sure to include the .WPM extension; otherwise, WordPerfect will no longer recognize the file as a macro.

Figure 13.2   **The macro for letter-closing**

```
Sincerely,



Macco Plastics, Inc.

Enclosure

cc:   R. Allen
      G. Berg
      K. Donnelly
      A. Hutton
      J. Murphy
```

RUNNING A MACRO

When you run (play back) a macro, the keystrokes you stored in the macro are repeated. To run a macro:

- Position the cursor at the place where you want the macro to run.

- Press the Macro keys, Alt-F10.

- Type the macro name. Do not type the .WPM extension when prompted for the macro name.

- Press Enter to run the macro. There is no message that tells you when the macro has finished running. To stop a macro while it is running, press the Cancel key, F1.

With the typing area cleared, follow these steps at your computer:

1. Press **Alt-F10** (Macro). WordPerfect prompts you to name the existing macro file:

   Macro:

2. Type **myformat** (the name you assigned to the macro), and press **Enter**. (If that file is unavailable, insert the Data Disk in drive A, press **Enter**, and type **a:xmyforma**.) The stored keystrokes are played back.

3. Type **Frank Williams** and press **Enter** to move to the next line.

4. Type **80 Wellington Street** and press **Enter**.

5. Type **Toronto, Ontario M5K 1A2** and press **Enter** twice to end the line and skip a blank line.

6. Type **Dear Frank:** and press **Enter** twice.

7. Retrieve the document CONTRACT.LRN from the Data Disk using **Shift-F10**. The stored text is placed at the cursor position.

 RUNNING A MACRO WITH A PAUSE

The letter is not quite complete; it still needs a closing. You can quickly add the closing by running the MYCLOSE macro, following these steps at your computer:

1. Position the cursor at the bottom of the document.

2. Press Alt-F10 (Macro), and type **myclose**. If that file is unavailable, type **a:xmyclose**.

3. Press **Enter** to run the closing macro. Although there is no prompt or message, the macro pauses to allow you to type the name of the person sending the letter.

4. Type **Morgan D. Hamilton** and press **Enter**. The macro pauses again to allow you to type the title.

5. Type **Vice President** and press **Enter**. The rest of the macro plays itself out.

6. Examine the completed letter. Compare it to the one shown in Figure 13.3.

7. Save the document as MYCOVLET.LRN. Press **F10** to keep the document in the typing area.

USING THE ALT KEY TO NAME A MACRO

You know that macro file names can contain up to eight characters. You can also name a macro by pressing the Alt key followed by a single letter when prompted for the macro name. The advantage of naming a macro using the Alt-letter combination is that you run the macro by pressing only those two keys: You simply hold down the Alt key and type the single letter. In contrast, to start a macro without this shortcut, you must press the Macro keys (Alt-F10), type the full file name, and press Enter.

Figure 13.3 **The letter completed by combining macros and stored text**

```
                          MACCO PLASTICS, INC.
                         2345 Industrial Parkway
                           Nashua, NH  03060


        (Today's Date)


        Frank Williams
        80 Wellington Street
        Toronto, Ontario M5K 1A2

        Dear Frank:

        Welcome to our growing list of satisfied clients.  You
        have indeed made a wise  buying  decision.  You can
        depend on us for fast, reliable, and efficient service.
        As a vendor for more than eight years, we can offer you
        a wide range of experience in the field.

        Enclosed are two  copies of  your maintenance contract
        covering the system you recently purchased from us.  If
        you experience  any problems  with your system, contact
        Bob Taylor, Customer Service.  He will  have one of our
        service representatives call on you.

        Sincerely,


        Morgan D. Hamilton
        Vice President
        Macco Plastics, Inc.

        Enclosure

        cc:  R. Allen
             G. Berg
             K. Donnelly
             A. Hutton
             J. Murphy
```

The disadvantage of naming macros using the Alt-letter combination is that the names are not very descriptive. When using these single-letter names, try to make them as obvious as possible. For example, use *C* for a letter-closing macro, *P* for a print macro, and so on.

In the following activity, you will create a macro that prints a letter in draft mode. Before you begin the activity, the letter shown in Figure 13.3 should be in the typing area. (If it is not available, retrieve the file XMYCOVLE.LRN from the Data Disk.)

1. Press **Ctrl-F10** (Macro Define). You see the prompt

   `Define macro:`

2. Press **Alt-P** to name the macro. Notice the prompt

   `Description:`

3. Press **Enter** to bypass the optional description. The flashing message tells you that the recorder is now on:

   `Macro Def`

4. Press **Shift-F7** to display the Print menu, choose **T - Text** Quality to display the Text Quality menu, choose **2 D**raft, and choose **1 - F**ull Document to tell the macro how you want to print the letter.

5. Press **Ctrl-F10** (Macro Define). The flashing prompt disappears from the screen, signaling the end of the macro recording session.

When you use the Alt-letter combination to name a macro, the macro file is saved to the disk just as if you had typed *alt* plus the letter. The file you just created by pressing Alt-P is saved by Word-Perfect as *ALTP.WPM*.

EDITING A MACRO

What if you have made some mistakes in recording your macro, or you would simply like to change it? WordPerfect's Macro Editor makes it possible for you to edit a macro that you've already created, saving you the time and trouble of deleting the faulty macro and starting from scratch.

EDITING TEXT IN THE MACRO

If you try to define a new macro by a name that already exists, WordPerfect displays a message telling you that the macro is already defined, along with the following options prompt:

```
1 Replace; 2 Edit: 3 Description: 0
```

If you choose *Replace*, then the original macro is deleted and the macro definition process starts again. If you choose *Edit*, then the cursor is placed in the Macro Editor so you can change the existing macro. If you choose *Description*, you can change the description of the existing macro *without* modifying what the macro does.

With the document MYCOVLET.LRN in the typing area, follow these steps at your computer:

1. Press **Ctrl-F10** (Macro Define). WordPerfect prompts

```
Define macro:
```

2. Type **myclose** and press **Enter**. Notice the prompt

```
MYCLOSE.WPM Already Exists:
1 Replace; 2 Edit, 3 Description: 0
```

3. Choose **2 E**dit. The Macro Editor appears. (See Figure 13.4.)

Figure 13.4   **The Macro Editor**

```
Macro: Action

     File              MYCLOSE.WPM

     Description

    ┌──────────────────────────────────────────────┐
    │{Enter}                                        │
    │Sincerely,{Enter}                              │
    │{Enter}                                        │
    │{Enter}                                        │
    │{Enter}                                        │
    │{PAUSE}{Enter}                                 │
    │{PAUSE}{Enter}                                 │
    │Macco·Plastics,·Inc.{Enter}                    │
    │{Enter}                                        │
    │Enclosure{Enter}                               │
    │{Enter}                                        │
    │cc:{Tab}R.·Allen{Enter}                        │
    │{Tab}G.·Berg{Enter}                            │
    │{Tab}K.·Donnelly{Enter}                        │
    │{Tab}A.·Hutton{Enter}                          │
    └──────────────────────────────────────────────┘

Ctrl-PgUp for macro commands;   Press Exit when done
```

4. Move to the *R* in *R. Allen*.

5. Press **Del** eight times to delete *R. Allen*.

6. Type **A. Archer**, the new closing name.

7. Move the cursor to the bottom of the screen.

8. Press **Tab**. The cursor moves one tab stop to the right. Suppose that what you wanted to do, however, was to insert a {Tab} code into the macro.

9. Press **Backspace**.

10. Press **Ctrl-V** and press **Tab** to insert a {Tab} code into the macro.

11. Type **M. Short**.

12. Press **Ctrl-V** and press **Enter** to insert an {Enter} code into the macro.

When editing a macro, keep in mind the following:

- Text is inserted and deleted the same way as in the typing area. For example, the arrow keys, Del, and Backspace can be used in the usual manner.

- For most features and commands, you press the corresponding key to insert the feature or command in the macro. For example, press F10 to insert the Save command into the macro.

- To include the Exit and Cancel features in your macro, as well as Tab, Enter, and the cursor-movement keys, you must first press Ctrl-V, and then press the appropriate key. If you press F7 (Exit) without first pressing Ctrl-V, you will simply exit the Macro Editor.

 ## SOUNDING THE BELL WHEN THE MACRO PAUSES

You can set up your macro to make your computer beep when the macro pauses. You access the Bell command through the Macro Commands menu (Ctrl-PgUp) while in the Macro Editor.

With the macro MYCLOSE.WPM in the Macro Editor, follow these steps at your computer:

1. Move to the beginning of the first line that contains a {PAUSE} code.

2. Press **Ctrl-PgUp** to display a list of commands in the upper-right corner.

3. Highlight *{BELL}* (press ↓ twice).

4. Press **Enter** to insert the Bell command in the macro.

PRACTICE YOUR SKILLS

1. Insert another {BELL} before the second pause. You must press **Ctrl-PgUp** again to bring up the command list.

2. Press **F7** when you are done, to save your changes and return to the typing area.

EDITING THE CLOSING AND RUNNING THE NEW CLOSING MACRO

Now that you've edited the closing macro so it contains a bell, let's delete the old closing and run the macro again.

Follow these steps at your computer:

1. Move to the blank line above *Sincerely,* near the bottom of the letter.

2. Block and highlight the text designated as the closing, beginning with the blank line, through the list of names ending with *J. Murphy.*

3. Delete the closing.

4. Run the macro MYCLOSE.WPM by pressing **Alt-F10**. The computer beeps when the macro pauses.

5. Type **Morgan D. Hamilton** and press **Enter** to release the pause. The next bell sounds.

6. Type **Vice President** and press **Enter**. The rest of the macro is performed.

7. Examine the changes caused by the new macro.

8. Use **F7** to update the document. Type **Y** to replace the existing document and clear the typing area.

PRACTICE YOUR SKILLS

This section gives you the opportunity to practice the skills you just learned. You will create a macro for creating a form, as shown in Figure 13.5. This macro will contain pauses to allow the user to type information from the keyboard. You can see the final form in Figure 13.6.

Figure 13.5   **The form stored in the macro MYFORM.WPM**

```
                          NOTIFICATION OF SINGLE RELEASE

          RECORD #:                          A & R MAN:

          CG #:                              DATE:

          P.O. #:                            RELEASE DATE:

          WRITER(s):                         ALBUM #:

          PRODUCED BY:                       PUBLISHER:

          ADDITIONAL INFORMATION:
```

Figure 13.6   **The completed form**

```
                          NOTIFICATION OF SINGLE RELEASE

          RECORD #:  1216                    A & R MAN:  Claude Hampton

          CG #:  13456                       DATE:  (Today's Date)

          P.O. #: 1023A                      RELEASE DATE:  June 11

          WRITER(s):  Tommie Russell         ALBUM #:  S-43481

          PRODUCED BY:  Clyde Brinkley       PUBLISHER:  Royal Music

          ADDITIONAL INFORMATION:  Final cut date May 5
```

With the typing area cleared, follow these steps at your computer:

1. Start the macro recording session by pressing the Macro Define keys and naming the macro file MYFORM. Bypass the description.

2. Change the line spacing to *2* through the Line Format menu.

3. While still in the Line Format menu, select **Tab Set**. Then do the following:

   - Press **Ctrl-End** to erase all tabs.

   - Set a left-aligned tab at Position 3.5".

   - Exit the Tab area and return to the document area.

4. Center and type the heading as seen in Figure 13.5.

5. Type the form following each colon (:) with two spaces and a pause. For example: Type **RECORD #**:

   - Insert two spaces after the colon.

   - Press **Ctrl-PgUp** and select **Pause**.

   - Press **Enter** once to release the pause.

   - Tab to the next title.

6. End the macro recording session.

7. Clear the typing area. Do *not* save the file again.

8. Run the macro **myform**.

9. Using Figure 13.6 as a guide, complete the form.

10. Save the document as MYPRAC13.LRN.

11. Print the completed form.

12. Clear the typing area.

When you have finished this activity, you might like to try another one that requires similar skills, yet is more challenging. Create the three macros shown in Figures 13.7, 13.8, and 13.9, and name them using the Alt key (refer to the figure captions). Running the macros creates the product form shown in Figure 13.10.

With the typing area cleared, follow these steps at your computer:

1. Create a macro, named by pressing **Alt-A**, to store the heading seen in Figure 13.7. Insert a pause after the colon (:).

Figure 13.7   **The file ALTA.WPM**

```
                              MACCO PLASTICS INC.
                            2345 Industrial Parkway
                              Nashua, NH  03060
                               (603) 223-5678
        TO:
```

Figure 13.8   **The file ALTB.WPM**

```
                                                   NEW PRODUCT RELEASE
        ----------------------------------------------------------------
        PRODUCT #:
                                     Expected Release    Price per
        Name:                        Date:               Unit: $

        Purpose/Description:
```

Figure 13.9   **The file ALTC.WPM**

```
        PREFERRED CUSTOMER PRICING INFORMATION
        ----------------------------------------------------------------
            Macco Plastics  Inc. sincerely  appreciates the patronage of
            all of our  customers   and  holds  special  customers  like
            _____  in  high  regard.   Therefore, the introductory
            prices above have  been  discounted  an  additional _____
            percent.

            As always,  we encourage  your comments  and look forward to
            serving you for years to come.
```

2. Clear the typing area.

3. Create the product-announcement form seen in Figure 13.8, naming the macro by pressing **Alt-B**. As you do so:

    *   Set left-aligned tab stops for the *Expected Release Date:* and *Price Per Unit: $* lines.

Figure 13.10   **The assembled document MYOPT13.LRN**

```
                        MACCO PLASTICS INC.
                      2345 Industrial Parkway
                        Nashua, NH  03060
                         (603) 223-5678
      TO:  Bonakin Distributors
           1099 Hoffman Place
           Augusta, Georgia  30901

                                       NEW PRODUCT RELEASE
      -----------------------------------------------------------------
      PRODUCT #: 1
                              Expected Release    Price per
      Name: Plasti-cote Trays     Date: June      Unit: $3.20 ea.

      Purpose/Description: These  trays  will  fill  the  need  for an
      inexpensive,  durable,  attractive  tray  for  carrying  food in
      cafeterias.  Color  selections  are:   orange, yellow, brown, and
      red.   The  dimensions are 18" by  24" and the  recommended  load
      limit is three pounds.

                                       NEW PRODUCT RELEASE
      -----------------------------------------------------------------
      PRODUCT #: 2
                              Expected Release    Price per
      Name: Chug                  Date: April     Unit: $.10 ea.

      Purpose/Description: Chugs  are  pieces of  molded  plastic that
      hold up  shelving units,  most commonly  inside kitchen cabinets.
      Several  models  will  be  available  for  different  placements:
      corner, mid-shelf, and end, as  well as chugs that fasten a shelf
      in place versus those on which the shelf lies.

      PREFERRED CUSTOMER PRICING INFORMATION
      -----------------------------------------------------------------
          Macco Plastics  Inc. sincerely  appreciates the patronage of
          all of our  customers and  holds  special  customers  like
          Bonakin  Distributors  in  high regard.   Therefore,  the
          introductory prices above have been discounted an additional
          fifteen percent.

          As always,  we encourage  your comments  and look forward to
          serving you for years to come.
```

- Insert pauses after each colon (:).

4. Clear the typing area.

5. Create the pricing policy seen in Figure 13.9, naming the macro by pressing **Alt-C**. Include pauses for typing the customer name and percent discounted.

6. Clear the typing area.

7. Combine running the macros and typing text to assemble the final document shown in Figure 13.10. (Hint: To run a macro named using the Alt key, press Alt plus the letter used in the macro name. You need not press Alt-F10.)

8. Print the completed document, and compare your printout to Figure 13.10.

9. Save the document as MYOPT13.LRN.

CHAPTER SUMMARY

In this chapter you learned how to create, name, run, and edit macros to help you use your word-processing time more efficiently. You also learned how to prompt the macro user by making the computer beep every time the macro pauses.

Here's a quick technique reference for Chapter 13:

Feature or Action	How to Do It
Record a macro	**Ctrl-F10** (Macro Define), type the macro name, **Enter**, type a description and/or **Enter**, press the keys you want to record, **F7** (Exit)
Insert a Pause	While recording keystrokes, **Ctrl-PgUp** (Macro Commands), **1 P**ause, **Enter**
Run a macro	Position the cursor, **Alt-F10** (Macro), <macro name>, **Enter**; or press **Alt** and the associated letter
Stop a macro while it is running	**F1** (Cancel)
Use Alt to name macros	**Ctrl-F10** (Macro Define), **Alt-letter**, continue recording the macro
Edit a macro	**Ctrl-F10** (Macro Define), <macro name>, **Enter**, **2 E**dit, perform the edits, **F7**

Congratulations! You have arrived at the end of this book. You've learned to use all of WordPerfect's basic features plus some that are considerably more sophisticated. Now more than ever, it bears repeating that practice is the best way to get comfortable with everything you've learned. That's why you should feel free to review the material in this book whenever you have a question. This was the main reason for keeping the original Data Disk files intact. So, remember to keep your Data Disk in a safe place, and good luck as you continue using your new-found skills on your own WordPerfect documents.

APPENDIX A: INSTALLING WORDPERFECT

Using
WordPerfect's
Installation
Program

This appendix shows you how to install WordPerfect on your computer's hard disk using WordPerfect's own installation program. You will be installing the program onto a directory called C:\WP51, which will be created during the installation process.

USING WORDPERFECT'S INSTALLATION PROGRAM

WordPerfect's installation program, INSTALL.EXE, is designed to simplify the installation process by providing you with prompts and menus. If you follow these prompts and menus carefully, then you will find this procedure straightforward.

Note: WordPerfect is so designed that you must run INSTALL.EXE to install WordPerfect properly. Do not attempt to install WordPerfect without using the installation program.

Follow these steps at your computer:

1. Turn on your computer. (If necessary, refer to your computer manual for the correct procedure.) You should see a DOS prompt such as C\, C:\, or C:\>.

2. Find the WordPerfect 5.1 disk labeled "Install/Learn/Utilities 1," and insert it in your computer's drive A or B, depending on the size of the disk.

3. Type **A:** or **B:** (depending on your choice in Step 2) and press **Enter** to access drive A or B.

4. Type **install** and press **Enter** to run the installation program. A sign-on screen is displayed.

5. Press **Enter** to continue the installation. If you are asked whether you have a color monitor, type **Y** for yes or **N** for no. The installation program then prompts you to indicate whether you are installing the program on a hard disk.

6. Type **Y** to install the program to your computer's hard disk. The main installation menu (Figure A.1) is displayed; you may see additional options depending on when your copy of WordPerfect was produced.

7. Choose **1 - B**asic by typing **1** or **B**. A series of screen prompts is displayed, asking you questions about installing WordPerfect's various optical components and giving you a brief description of each.

8. Follow each screen prompt. Type **Y** to answer a question, place the requested disk in drive A or B, then press **Enter** to continue.

After you've copied all the disks, the program automatically takes you through more installation procedures, which are described in the following sections.

Figure A.1   **Main Installation menu**

```
Installation
    1 - Basic       Perform a standard installation to C:\WP51.

    2 - Custom      Perform a customized installation.  (User selected
                    directories.)

    3 - Network     Perform a customized installation onto a network.
                    (To be performed by the network supervisor.)

    4 - Printer     Install updated Printer (.ALL) File.

    5 - Update      Install updated program file(s).

    6 - Copy Disks  Install every file from an installation diskette to a
                    specified location.  (Useful for installing all the
                    Printer (.ALL) Files.)




Selection: 1
```

MODIFYING THE CONFIG.SYS FILE

Most DOS files tell your system what to do; CONFIG.SYS tells your system how to do it. One piece of information contained in this file is the maximum number of files that can be opened at any one time. For WordPerfect to run correctly, the file must allow for at least 20 files to be open simultaneously.

During the next step in the installation process, the program automatically checks the contents of CONFIG.SYS. If the file already allows for enough files to be open, a message indicates that this is so; press any key to continue. If CONFIG.SYS does not exist or does not allow for enough files to be open at once, WordPerfect will let you know. Type **Y** as each question is posed; the installation program will create or modify your CONFIG.SYS file automatically.

MODIFYING THE AUTOEXEC.BAT FILE

Another file that is checked automatically during the installation process is AUTOEXEC.BAT. This file tells your computer what to do every time you turn it on. It also tells your system where it can find certain files, such as your WordPerfect program.

If your system does not contain AUTOEXEC.BAT, one is created for you in your root directory during the installation process. In any case, the installation program next tells your system where it can find WordPerfect. To do this, the instruction

```
PATH=C:\WP51
```

or

```
;C:\WP51;
```

is automatically added to (or created with) the AUTOEXEC.BAT file.

 INSTALLING PRINTERS

The next step is to tell WordPerfect what kind of printer (or printers) you will be using. As the screen instructs you to do so, follow these steps at your computer:

1. Insert the "Printer 1" disk into drive A or B and press **Enter**. You will see a list of printers that WordPerfect can use.

2. Press **PgDn** or **PgUp** to scroll through the list. If your printer is not in the list, check your printer manual to see if it recommends specifying a compatible make and model. Some printers are marked with an asterisk (*) in the list of printers, indicating that they are not available. If your printer is listed twice, once with the asterisk and again without it, select the one without the asterisk.

3. Once you have found your printer (or one compatible with it) type its number and press **Enter** to select it. WordPerfect asks you to confirm your selection.

4. Type **Y** to confirm. You are asked if you would like to install the printer's .ALL file, which contains information needed to use your printer with WordPerfect.

5. Type **Y** and follow the instructions displayed on the screen. Periodically, you will be asked to insert a new disk. Remember to press **Enter** as you finish swapping disks. You will then be asked if you want to install another printer.

6. If you will be using more than one printer, type **Y** and repeat the above steps for selecting a printer. If you will be using only one printer, type **N**. A screen is displayed, which asks for your customer registration number.

7. Type your customer registration number (optional), and press **Enter** to continue. Some printer information is displayed.

8. If your printer is already connected to your system, press **Shift-PrtSc** to print a copy of the printer information screen.

9. Press any key to exit the screen.

COMPLETING THE INSTALLATION

When the installation is completed, a message to this effect will be displayed. Because your CONFIG.SYS and AUTOEXEC.BAT files have been modified or created during the installation process, you'll need to restart your computer for those modifications to be put into effect.

Follow these steps at your computer:

1. Remove any floppy disks from your drives.

2. Press **Ctrl-Alt-Del** to restart your system.

Now, you're ready to turn to Chapter 1 and begin learning how to use WordPerfect 5.1!

APPENDIX B: WORDPERFECT'S HELP SYSTEM

Using Help

Context-Sensitive
Help

WordPerfect offers a Help system that you can use when you are working on your own in the program. This Help system provides you with information on almost all of WordPerfect's commands, menus, and cursor movements.

USING HELP

To access the Help feature, follow these steps at your computer:

1. From the WordPerfect typing area, press **F3** (Help). The opening Help screen is displayed (Figure B.1). From this screen, you can type any letter to see a list of features beginning with that letter, or type a function key or key combination to see information about what that key does in WordPerfect.

2. Type **a** to see a list of features whose name begins with that letter (Figure B.2).

3. There are more features than can fit on a screen, so type **a** again to see more features beginning with *a*.

4. Press **Shift-F1** to see information about the WordPerfect Setup options, and select **6 - L**ocation of Files to see information about the Location of Files option.

5. Press **Enter** to return to the typing area. (Don't press F1 or F7, WordPerfect's usual keys for returning to the typing area; if you do, you'll just see Help screens for Cancel and Exit, respectively.)

Figure B.1   **The opening Help screen**

```
Help                                              WP 5.1    06/29/90


        Press any letter to get an alphabetical list of features.

             The list will include the features that start with that letter,
             along with the name of the key where the feature is found.  You
             can then press that key to get a description of how the feature
             works.

        Press any function key to get information about the use of the key.

             Some keys may let you choose from a menu to get more information
             about various options.  Press HELP again to display the template.







Selection: 0                                      (Press ENTER to exit Help)
```

Figure B.2   **Help's alphabetized features list**

```
Features [A]                             WordPerfect Key    Keystrokes

Absolute Tab Settings                    Format             Shft-F8,1,8,t,1
Acceleration Factor (Mouse)              Setup              Shft-F1,1,5
Add Password                             Text In/Out        Ctrl-F5,2
Additional Printers                      Print              Shft-F7,s,2
Advance (To Position, Line, etc.)        Format             Shft-F8,4,1
Advanced Macro Commands (Macro Editor)   Macro Commands     Ctrl-PgUp
Advanced Merge Codes                     Merge Codes        Shft-F9,6
Align/Decimal Character                  Format             Shft-F8,4,3
Align Text on Tabs                       Tab Align          Ctrl-F6
Alphabetize Text                         Merge/Sort         Ctrl-F9,2
Alt/Ctrl Key Mapping                     Setup              Shft-F1,5
Alt-=                                    Menu Bar           Alt-=
Appearance of Printed Text               Font               Ctrl-F8
Append Text to a File (Block On)         Move               Ctrl-F4,1-3,4
Append to Clipboard (Block On)           Shell              Ctrl-F1,3
ASCII Text File                          Text In/Out        Ctrl-F5,1
Assign Keys                              Setup              Shft-F1,5
Assign Variable                          Macro Commands     Ctrl-PgUp
Attributes, Printed                      Font               Ctrl-F8
Attributes, Screen                       Setup              Shft-F1,2,1
More... Press a to continue.

Selection: 0                                       (Press ENTER to exit Help)
```

6. Press **F3** twice to see a keyboard template showing all of Word-Perfect's function-key commands (Figure B.3). The template you see may differ from the one shown in the figure. You can see this template from any Help screen by pressing F3.

7. Press **Enter** to return to the typing area.

CONTEXT-SENSITIVE HELP

Another way to obtain specific information about a feature is to use *context-sensitive* Help. Context-sensitive Help enables you to obtain help from anywhere in the program, not just from the main typing area. For example, if you have displayed a menu, press F3 to get information about that menu.

Use the same method to exit from context-sensitive Help that you would use to exit from general Help: press Enter. This brings you back to where you were before you accessed Help.

Figure B.3   **Help's keyboard template**

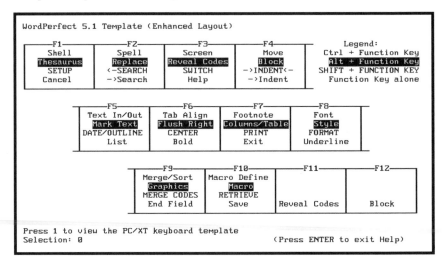

APPENDIX C:
FILE CONVERSION

Converting a
Document from
Another Word
Processor to
WordPerfect
Format

Saving a
WordPerfect 5.1 File
in WordPerfect 5.0
or 4.2 Format

This appendix shows you how to transfer information between WordPerfect and other programs with WordPerfect's Convert program. Table C.1 lists the available file conversions.

Table C.1   **Convert Program Options**

Option	Description
1 WordPerfect to another format	Converts a WordPerfect file to one of the following formats: Revisable-Form, Final-Form, Navy DIF (Data Interchange Format), WordStar 3.3, MultiMate Advantage II, Seven-Bit Transfer Format, or ASCII text file. It also can convert a WordPerfect secondary (Merge) file to a Spreadsheet DIF file.
2 Revisable-Form-Text and 3 Final-Form-Text (IBM DCA Format) to WordPerfect	Converts DCA files (used by some mainframes) to WordPerfect.
4 Navy DIF Standard to WordPerfect	Converts the Navy Data Interchange Format (DIF), a standard method of storing spreadsheet data used by Lotus 1-2-3, to WordPerfect.
5 WordStar 3.3 to WordPerfect	Converts WordStar, another word-processing program, to WordPerfect.
6 MultiMate Advantage II to WordPerfect	Converts MultiMate, another word-processing program, to WordPerfect.
7 Seven-Bit Transfer Format to WordPerfect	A useful format when transferring files over a modem or line that transfers only seven bits.
8 WordPerfect 4.2 to WordPerfect 5.1	Converts a WordPerfect 4.2 document to 5.1. See "Saving a WordPerfect 5.1 File in WordPerfect 5.0 or 4.2 Format," just ahead, on conversions in the other direction.
9 Mail Merge to WordPerfect Secondary Merge	Useful with dBASE, Lotus 1-2-3, and other mail-merge files.

Option	Description
A Spreadsheet DIF to WordPerfect Secondary Merge	Converts a spreadsheet file into a WordPerfect secondary (Merge) file.
B Word 4.0 to WordPerfect	Converts Microsoft Word 4.0, another word-processing program, to WordPerfect.

CONVERTING A DOCUMENT FROM ANOTHER WORD PROCESSOR TO WORDPERFECT FORMAT

Before you convert files, you should be at the DOS prompt. To convert a document from another word processor:

- From the root directory, type cd wp51 and press Enter to change to the subdirectory where your WordPerfect program is located.

- Type convert and press Enter to run the conversion utility. The utility prompts you to name the file to be converted:

  Name of Input File?

- Type the name of the file to be converted, and press Enter. Remember to include the full path if the file is in a different drive or directory. Also, remember to type the file extension, the last three characters in the file name. The utility prompts you to name a new file for your converted document.

  Name of Output File?

- Type the file name for the converted file, and press Enter. This will display the Conversion menu (Figure C.1).

- From the Conversion menu, type the menu number or bold letter to choose the option that describes the conversion you would like to perform. If you are converting to WordPerfect, a message tells you that the input file (from the program) has been converted to the output file (in WordPerfect 5.1 format). If you are converting from WordPerfect to another program, you will see a new menu of possible file formats; type the menu number or letter of the desired format.

Figure C.1   **The Conversion menu**

```
Name of Input File? a:productn.doc
Name of Output File? a:productn

0 EXIT
1 WordPerfect to another format
2 Revisable-Form-Text (IBM DCA Format) to WordPerfect
3 Final-Form-Text (IBM DCA Format) to WordPerfect
4 Navy DIF Standard to WordPerfect
5 WordStar 3.3 to WordPerfect
6 MultiMate Advantage II to WordPerfect
7 Seven-Bit Transfer Format to WordPerfect
8 WordPerfect 4.2 to WordPerfect 5.1
9 Mail Merge to WordPerfect Secondary Merge
A Spreadsheet DIF to WordPerfect Secondary Merge
B Word 4.0 to WordPerfect
C DisplayWrite to WordPerfect

Enter number of Conversion desired
```

SAVING A WORDPERFECT 5.1 FILE IN WORDPERFECT 5.0 OR 4.2 FORMAT

To save a WordPerfect 5.1 document in WordPerfect 5.0 or 4.2 format, use the Text In/Out function, Ctrl-F5, choose 3 Save As, and select the desired format. This feature saves the document on your screen in the new format; it can then be retrieved within WordPerfect 5.0 or 4.2.

To use a WordPerfect 4.2 or 5.0 document in WordPerfect 5.1, simply retrieve it the same way you retrieve a WordPerfect 5.1 document.

INDEX

■ TO RECEIVE 3$\frac{1}{2}$-INCH DISK(S)

The Ziff-Davis Press software contained on the 5$\frac{1}{4}$-inch disk(s) included with this book is also available in 3$\frac{1}{2}$-inch (720k) format. If you would like to receive the software in the 3$\frac{1}{2}$-inch format, please return the 5$\frac{1}{4}$-inch disk(s) with your name and address to:

Disk Exchange
Ziff-Davis Press
5903 Christie Avenue
Emeryville, CA 94608